The Power of Portfolios

What Children Can Teach Us About Learning and Assessment

Elizabeth A. Hebert

JOSSEY-BASS
A Wiley Company
San Francisco

Published by

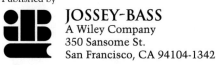

JOSSEY-BASS
A Wiley Company
350 Sansome St.
San Francisco, CA 94104-1342

www.josseybass.com

Some portions of the Conclusion previously appeared in:
Hebert, E. A. "Lessons Learned About Student Portfolios." *Phi Delta Kappan*, April 1995, pp. 583–585. Reprinted by permission of *Phi Delta Kappan*.

Some portions of Chapter Seven and Chapter Ten previously appeared in:
Hebert, E. A. "Portfolios Invite Reflection—from Students and Staff." *Educational Leadership*, May 1992, 49 (8), pp. 58–61. Reprinted by permission of the Association for Supervision and Curriculum Development.
Hebert, E. A. "Design Matters: How School Environment Affects Children." *Educational Leadership*, September 1998, 56 (1), pp. 69–70. Reprinted by permission of the Association for Supervision and Curriculum Development.
Hebert, E., with Schultz, L. "The Power of Portfolios." *Educational Leadership*, April 1996, 53 (7), pp. 70–71. Reprinted by permission of the Association for Supervision and Curriculum Development.

Jossey-Bass books and products are available through most bookstores. To contact Jossey-Bass directly, call (888) 378-2537, fax to (800) 605-2665, or visit our website at www.josseybass.com.

Substantial discounts on bulk quantities of Jossey-Bass books are available to corporations, professional associations, and other organizations. For details and discount information, contact the special sales department at Jossey-Bass.

We at Jossey-Bass strive to use the most environmentally sensitive paper stocks available to us. Our publications are printed on acid-free recycled stock whenever possible, and our paper always meets or exceeds minimum GPO and EPA requirements.

Library of Congress Cataloging-in-Publication Data

Hebert, Elizabeth A. (Elizabeth Ann), date
  The power of portfolios : what children can teach us about learning and assessment / Elizabeth A. Hebert.—1st ed.
    p. cm.—(The Jossey-Bass education series)
Includes bibliographical references (p.   ) and index.
  ISBN 0-7879-5871-9 (alk. paper)
  1. Portfolios in education. 2. Educational tests and measurements. I. Title. II. Series.
LB1029.P67 H43 2001
  372.127—dc21   2001003792

HB Printing   10 9 8 7 6 5 4 3 2 1

The Jossey-Bass Education Series

Contents

Preface   ix

LESSON 1: Children Can Assess Their Own Learning   1

LESSON 2: Children Learn All the Time   11

LESSON 3: Teachers Learn All the Time, Too   23

LESSON 4: Getting Clear on Portfolio Purpose,
          Ownership, and Content   39

LESSON 5: Portfolios Encourage Children to Think
          About Their Learning   51

LESSON 6: Portfolios Respond to the Individual
          Needs of Students   63

LESSON 7: Designating a Space and Place for
          Gathering Memories   75

LESSON 8: A Celebration Connects Child, Portfolio,
          and Audience   85

LESSON 9: Teaching Parents How to Be Part of the
          Portfolio Conference   99

LESSON 10: Listening for Children's Meaning 111

LESSON 11: Creating a Language for Portfolios 121

CONCLUSION: Lessons Learned About Portfolios 131

Appendix: Philosophy of the Winnetka Public Schools 135

The Author 142

Bibliography 143

Index 149

PREFACE

Portfolios have been with us for a very long time. Those of us who grew up in the 1950s or earlier recognize portfolios as reincarnations of the large memory boxes or drawers where our parents collected starred spelling tests, lacy valentines, science fair posters, early attempts at poetry, and (of course) the obligatory set of plaster hands. Each item was selected by our parents because it represented our acquisition of a new skill or our feelings of accomplishment. Perhaps an entry was accompanied by a special notation of praise from a teacher or maybe it was placed in the box just because we did it.

We formed part of our identity from the contents of these memory boxes. We recognized each piece and its association with a particular time or experience. We shared these collections with grandparents to reinforce feelings of pride and we reexamined them on rainy days when friends were unavailable for play. Reflecting on the collection allowed us to attribute importance to these artifacts, and by extension to ourselves, as they gave witness to the story of our early school experiences.

Our parents couldn't possibly envision that these memory boxes would be the inspiration for an innovative way of thinking about children's learning. These collections, lovingly stored away on our behalf, are the genuine exemplar for documenting children's learning over time. But now these memory boxes have a different meaning. It's not purely private or personal, although the personal is what gives power to what they can mean.

Memory Boxes with New Intentions

What is the meaning of portfolios—these modern memory boxes—and why has their purpose changed? What portfolios can really accomplish is significant, but in many instances their full potential is not being reached. That is because portfolios are sometimes made into something they shouldn't be. Teachers who are uneasy with standardized tests and single-number characterizations of children's progress instinctively use portfolios in an attempt to prove their students' achievements. In these portfolios teachers select or they encourage their students to select what they believe is the child's best work and highest achievements and not necessarily what might be significant in the child's eyes or what reflects actual experiences. The teachers' hope is to supplement the narrower evaluation gleaned from standardized tests. But in doing so, the idea of a portfolio reflecting the realities of a child's education rather than only the high points has been lost.

This shift in function from memory box to standardized test supplement is an impediment to the portfolio's usefulness. The first problem is that the overriding expectation to serve as a qualitative companion to quantitative measures has placed a huge burden of expectation on portfolios—an expectation that cannot be fulfilled appropriately. A second, more serious problem is that fulfilling that first obligation sacrifices purposes and benefits unique to portfolios. Understanding what portfolios can do is what this book is about.

Portfolios as a Qualitative Companion

In experimenting with portfolios, teachers have understandably applied a format that is familiar to them. Organizing a portfolio that evidences a child's best work and a teacher's best teaching makes good

sense. But we need to ask ourselves where the coupling of *best work* and *portfolio* comes from? Why does it make such good sense to us?

It makes sense because many teachers naturally feel compelled to structure and standardize a child's portfolio to conform to the concept of evaluation we were raised on, that is, a single correct response. The notion of "one right answer" reinforces accustomed images of school and of the expected roles of teacher and student. This is how we experienced school as children. Teacher as knower, child as learner; teacher as in control, child as in compliance; teacher as posing questions, child as responding—these are some of the familiar dichotomies deeply rooted in our educational experience. And for that very reason, that is, just because this relationship is so viscerally familiar to us, we should scrutinize its obvious assumptions.

Examining and possibly changing our deeply ingrained attitudes and habits is a major hurdle to overcome. But until we confront the predictable attraction to our comfort zone, we will continue to superimpose a standardized template on portfolios or any other form of assessment without regard to its appropriateness. Dennie Wolf and her colleagues from Harvard Project Zero articulated the dilemma well:

> The design and implementation of alternative modes of assessment will entail nothing less than a wholesale transition from what we call a testing culture to an assessment culture . . . the observable differences in the form, the data, and the conduct of standardized testing and its alternatives are in no way superficial matters or mere surface features. They derive from radical differences in underlying conceptions of mind and of the evaluation process itself. Until we understand these differences and their network of consequences, we cannot develop new tools that will allow us to ensure that a wide range of students use their minds well [1991, p. 33].

The testing culture is well defined because we have devoted close to a century of experience toward the development of the form, data, and conduct of standardized testing. The content of evaluation and the explicit standards for achievement on those measures have been clearly defined. Most important, testing has a language and format that is understood by teachers, parents, and students alike.

We simply have not devoted that amount of time to discovering and developing the form, data, and conduct of portfolios. We've assumed a link to standardized tests without probing the correctness of that premise. The language of the testing culture has assimilated portfolios because no language about the use of portfolios exists. *Reliability, validity, quantitative judgment, measure*—these terms commonly describe standardized tests. They need to be redefined and clarified, however, when applied to portfolios (Gipps, 1999, p. 384; LeMahieu, Gitomer, and Eresh, 1995, pp. 11–28). In addition, we need to listen for the words that are unique to the portfolio experience.

Putting Portfolios to the Test

Schools across the country experimented with student portfolios in the 1980s. Those portfolio projects that approximated the ideals of the memory box received numerous criticisms. Evaluators of these projects were looking for a common measure to judge these portfolios— to find a way to compare one to another—to define the standard for a so-called good portfolio (Koretz and others, 1993, 1994; Mills, 1996; Sacks, 1999). In response many project designers promptly reworked portfolios to accommodate a quantitative ideology. The question was whether a substantially qualitative assessment tool could provide powerful and genuine insights into a child's learning as well as data about a student's comparative achievement.

Portfolios performed poorly on this test—and we shouldn't be surprised. The expectation that portfolios could yield a reliable and valid measure of one student's achievement as compared to another's, yet capture the uniqueness of a child's learning story, was unrealistic. This misguided attempt to fulfill incompatible goals is at the heart of the precarious future of portfolios. Standardized tests are a much better tool to measure *which child knows more*. Portfolios are—

or can be—the best vehicle to show us *what a child learns* and how schoolwork fits into that child's personal universe of knowledge. The combination of standardized tests and portfolios can provide a comprehensive assessment profile as well as invaluable insights into each child's process of learning.

It is a naive and unnecessary proposition to attempt to understand a child's learning by examining it through only one lens. We have multiple tools available to assist us to both measure and appreciate the complex dimensions of a child's learning. One tool is not better than another; rather each tool addresses different aspects of the learning profile. We need to know how to use each tool, however, so that we can understand the information gleaned and translate our insights into purposeful furthering of each child's learning.

Schools must be accountable to their communities. In support of that universal mandate teachers are encouraged to focus on what children can produce, and what can be seen and easily understood by parents and the community as students' progress toward meeting objective standards. Standardized tests are a good tool for this purpose. A longer view of the purposes of education, however, should urge us to be equally mindful of the process that children actually use in learning new skills or understanding new concepts. We should want to know how new knowledge changes children and how children incorporate new learning into everything else they know. This focus on a more far-reaching notion of lifelong accountability is just one of the unique benefits that portfolios can provide.

The Portfolio Advantage

Much has been written about the merits and drawbacks of standardized measures versus alternative modes of assessment, including portfolios. This ongoing debate has distracted us from attending to a more in-depth look at the unique benefits of portfolios. Too much time has been devoted to asking the wrong question ("What *should* a portfolio represent?") and not enough time has been directed to addressing the more substantive question of "What *can* a portfolio represent?"

In an insightful article that enumerates issues that will determine the success or failure of alternative assessments, Blaine Worthen states that "ultimately the success of alternative assessment will be judged by the persuasiveness of its internal rationales, rather than by external contrasts with traditional assessment. Criticisms of standardized testing are obviously less relevant to the future of new modes of assessment than are careful analyses of the most important advantages and drawbacks of those alternative assessment methods themselves" (1993, p. 446). The indigenous features of portfolios need to be brought to light. They must be understood as a generative tool for expanding and describing a child's learning.

More than a dozen years ago, at Crow Island School in Winnetka, Illinois, we began our long-term work with student portfolios. It still continues. Encouraging children to gather their work over their six years in elementary school so that they can see evidence of their own learning has taught us a lot. Understanding what the children and teachers think about portfolios sheds light on their fundamental value, as will be clear in succeeding chapters.

But it is important to remember that this has been the work of more than a decade. What problems did we confront and how did we resolve them? How did we learn to live with issues that seemingly couldn't be resolved? It began with very small steps toward very large ideas, and with a group of teachers who supported each other and who came to require of each other a school culture where ideas can be nurtured. That's when really important things can start to happen.

The Untidy Life of Ideas in a School Setting

In a school the life of an idea is filled with ambiguity, interruption, and chaos. Possibilities occur to teachers and principals at unexpected times—on the drive to school, in the middle of teaching a math lesson, during a conference with parents, or while putting children on the bus at the end of the day. With luck you have the opportunity to share a seed of an idea with a colleague in the hall-way or in the copier room. The act of talking about an idea—how-ever briefly—greatly increases the chances of a new thought taking root within that school.

Unlike problems that can be solved and routine emergencies that schools anticipate with procedures and drills, ideas follow a different path. The journey between inspiration and outcome is not direct. Ideas require long periods of incubation while our immediate ener-gies are focused on urgent interactions with children, parents, and teachers. Even when it is shared, a good idea requires time to traverse a school's circuitry in search of connection and energy. Further shared reflection generates additional possibilities and projects that only in retrospect can we identify as connected to the initial idea.

Our work with portfolios happened in just that way. We had an unclear notion of portfolios at the start. Influenced by Howard Gard-ner's *Frames of Mind: The Theory of Multiple Intelligences* (1983), we spent a great deal of time with projects that explored the multiple learning experiences of our students. We wanted to redesign our form for reporting pupil progress to parents. Both explorations proved to be directly related to our future work with portfolios, although we didn't realize it at that time. We now know that these ancillary proj-ects were not only necessary but added vitality to our growing inter-est in portfolios.

The following pages are an attempt to revisit over fourteen years of faculty conversations. The reader who is familiar with schools will recognize these chapters as an accurate portrayal of how the untidy life of ideas evolves in the school setting. The meandering rhythm of the beginning chapters is an honest depiction of how our faculty took the time to gather our thoughts and chart a direction.

We learn best through stories, so in many chapters the reader will find a vignette of school life. I hope these lessons will contribute to a new way of thinking about assessment in our schools. Here are the lessons that we have come to recognize as the internal rationales of student portfolios:

LESSON 1: Children Can Assess Their Own Learning

The most powerful reason for teaching children how to organize a portfolio of their work is to engage children in the assessment of their own learning. No other assessment tool can accomplish this goal as well.

LESSON 2: Children Learn All the Time

Children recognize a broader range of valued competencies, and attribute importance to them more evenly, than do their teachers. Teacher discussions of the multiple intelligences theory illuminated the many faces of learning and transformed our understanding of teaching and learning, and of ways to assess both.

LESSON 3: Teachers Learn All the Time, Too

In discussions about curriculum we often talk about providing large curricular concepts for children that offer many entries into a topic. Unfortunately, we don't always recognize that teachers require that same curricular model for growth. It's called good staff development. Redesigning our parent reporting form provided us with a rich project that stimulated our own multiple intelligences.

LESSON 4: Getting Clear on Portfolio Purpose, Ownership, and Content

"Whose portfolio is it?" is a question that must be addressed in order to know who will be making decisions about the contents of the collection. The transfer of ownership from teacher to child is a gradual process that evolves over time. Both teacher and child experience parallel stages of metacognitive insight that clarify issues of ownership. The ownership of the portfolio can be plotted along a continuum from exclusive teacher ownership to exclusive child ownership with an almost infinite number of intermediate stages.

LESSON 5: Portfolios Encourage Children to Think About Their Learning

The creation of portfolios and repeated interaction with them provides children with repetition and rehearsal of the act of self-reflection, discovery of strategies for learning, and affirmation of topics of interest. The presentation of a portfolio to a purposefully specified audience (say, parents) engages the child in a substantive conversation that further supports insights and self-knowledge required for the presentation of self to the world. As children become more aware of their strategies and dispositions for learning and learn how to exert control over these strategies, they become more confident learners.

LESSON 6: Portfolios Respond to the Individual Needs of Students

Children learn at different rates and demonstrate competence in a wide variety of subjects and projects. The portfolio is a tool that is responsive to a wide range of children's abilities. It serves as a means for the child to organize and assess present learning as well as set goals for future learning. The portfolio experience across the grade levels highlights development of emerging skills.

LESSON 7: Designating a Place and Space for Gathering Memories

Issues of space, accessibility, and innovative design of a school are directly connected to the child's portfolio experience. Thoughtfully designed spaces for learning have the power to evoke the dispositions required to engage in reflective assessment of learning. Establishing a school archive adds a sense of history to the portfolio and a place for our collective history as well.

LESSON 8: A Celebration Connects Child, Portfolio, and Audience

We needed a unifying experience that would consolidate all of our discussions and provide an experience for the children and parents that would clearly communicate the value we held for portfolios. Learning is an event worth celebrating, and children can be competent participants in that celebration. Portfolio conferences led by children have become for us the celebratory event that provides children with an authentic opportunity to relate their story of learning.

LESSON 9: Teaching Parents How to be Part of the Portfolio Conference

Each year we invite parents to a Portfolio Panel, where representative teachers from all grade levels discuss the reflective and assessment milestones achieved by children as they progress from Kindergarten to fifth grade. We recognize that the confidence and experience we've gained over these years is, in fact, more helpful to parents than if we had attempted to share our initial explorations and questions about portfolios many years ago. Now we are able to provide the appropriate scaffolding based on our years of conversations and direct experience so that the parents can hear their child's portfolio presentation and gain a more in-depth view of their child as a learner.

LESSON 10: Listening for Children's Meaning

As one fifth grade student reflects on her six-year archive, she connects prior and present learning experiences that describe and explain her dispositions for learning and future career goals as well. The underlying coherence and organization of the portfolio can only be expressed by its creator. Linkages between early learning experiences and present projects affirm the value of the portfolio as a vital collection of topics of interest and skills attained.

LESSON 11: Creating a Language for Portfolios

New language signals new thinking that in turn generates new language. There are words and phrases that have emerged in our language over the years that we commonly associate with the portfolio experience. We use these words and phrases with each other, with children, and with parents so as to define portfolios and to communicate what portfolios can do.

CONCLUSION: LESSONS LEARNED ABOUT STUDENT PORTFOLIOS

A final chapter sums up and weaves together the lessons we have learned from the portfolio process. The most significant benefits of portfolios for children, for teachers, and for parents are highlighted.

This Book Is a Portfolio

This book is not just about the portfolio concept—it is a portfolio in itself. It tells the story of my learning about portfolios and, hopefully it is a story that will help you learn about portfolios as well.

I confront a file drawer in disarray.

As I thumb through folders of old memos and early writings I realize these records comprise my portfolio. It is a collection that chronicles my developing understanding about a single topic—the making of student portfolios. I reread this accumulation of documents in the same way, I now know, that children review their portfolios. I don't recognize some pieces as mine because I don't remember thinking that thought or using those words. But here they are with my name on them—reminding me of important episodes in my learning.

My portfolio is also a collective portfolio. As principal of an elementary school, I have been inspired and influenced by the innovative ideas of an outstanding group of teachers and countless conversations with children. The open exchange that fosters the growth of ideas is present here. Each of us would have different ways of organizing those ideas, which is the very nature of a portfolio.

As I sort this jumbled yet coherent collection, I am struck by the many different organizational possibilities. Slowly and carefully I intuit a scaffolding that will allow me to make meaning out of this accumulation. Yes, that's the underlying purpose—to make meaningful connections. As I browse through these materials, I come across articles I have written in which I was able to make important connections among the many fragments of my observations, conversations, intuitions, and experiences. It satisfies me to retrace what I now understand was a purposeful development of my thinking.

Some of the ostensibly unrelated contents of my portfolio—articles about multiple intelligences theory, a videotape of a child playing golf, classroom schedules, drafts of parent reporting forms, a taxi receipt from a Washington, D.C., conference, and scribbled vignettes of daily life at Crow Island School all make sense to me now as meaningful items in the evolution of my understanding. I realize that only I can make the associations that connect the items that influenced my learning. That's an important idea. It has taken me all these years to really comprehend that it's not the content of the portfolio that matters—it's the meaning associated with the content. And the meaning can only be attributed by the portfolio creator. That's a very different notion of how to assess a child's work than the one I grew up with, that is, that my achievements were evaluated by teachers or judged by scores I received on standardized tests.

Portfolios encourage a unique response to the question "What have I learned?" because the response is personal and self-generated. Collecting and reflecting on self-selected evidence of learning allows the portfolio maker to assume genuine responsibility for both assessing learning and expressing that assessment to others who have a stake in it—teachers, parents, and colearners. An external and less personal, but also valid, evaluation of learning is gleaned through a variety of testing instruments. These capture a child's demonstration of specified learning objectives as stated by the school. They show the degree to which these objectives are met. Each of these ap-proaches to assessment—portfolios and standardized tests—yields different yet essential information about the child's learning and growth. Because their purposes and products are very different they shouldn't be compared.

A portfolio can be understood as a learning repository that con-tains evidence of skills attained over time, topics of interest, a his-tory of what was thought to be important and why. But that notion is of portfolio in its dormant state. There is also an active state for portfolio, an ongoing and generative interaction between the col-lection and the collector. This interaction represents one of many unrecognized dimensions of portfolios.

My portfolio is an invaluable resource in clarifying my early thoughts about portfolio development and helping me to imagine and shape future projects. Beyond that mature comprehension of what this collection can represent, I too experience the same child-like feelings of satisfaction voiced so well by one student as she re-flected upon her portfolio: "I like showing myself what I have done."

Over the years I have observed hundreds of children constructing their individual portfolios and creating a story about their learning rel-evant to its contents. I have noted how they attribute significance to particular pieces of their learning through the wording and attach-ment of what we call a "reflection tag"—a brief statement like the ones you'll see preceding the lessons here. With this book, I have an opportunity to engage in that same task. And just as the children have shown me how to do it, I will organize the content of my port-folio to best tell the story of my learning.

Winnetka, Illinois   Elizabeth A. Hebert
June 2001

Reflection Tag

I chose this piece for my portfolio because . . .

Tim's story—the one that opens this chapter—is a good place
to begin. It pulls all the pieces of this portfolio together in a
coherent way. Tim was only in second grade when he voiced
a memorable connection between his prior and present learning.
Tim taught me that children *can* assess their own learning. He
understood the "deep structure" of portfolio . . . and now so do I.

LESSON 1

Children Can Assess
Their Own Learning

A delegation of second graders, each with a red-roped archival envelope secured under one arm, was walking purposefully down the hallway in the direction of the first grade classrooms. I observed their decisive stride and suspected their mission. I immediately extricated myself from an unscheduled parent conference in the hallway and quickened my pace to catch up with this group of four students and their teacher. They had just taken their seats on the window benches when I arrived. The first graders gathered on the rug at the feet of their wiser elders. No teacher needed to remind these first graders of rugtime posture or behavior—they wanted to hear what these second graders had to say.

It was the first week in May and the first grade students were preparing for their very first Portfolio Conference with their parents. It had occurred to their teacher that it would be helpful for novice chroniclers to hear firsthand from some slightly older students how they might go about organizing their portfolios. Children talking to children about common experiences has proven to be a very powerful resource.

At first, each of the four second graders began by randomly enumerating the contents of their collection. Slightly unsure of how to communicate their organizational thinking, they provided a truncated rationale as to why these particular selections of their work were included. However, the rapt attention of the first graders made these second graders realize the importance of their remarks. They delved into their portfolios and their minds for the examples and the words that would make sense. They shifted naturally from the what to the why of portfolios. Listening for children's meaning is a far easier task for a child than for an adult. The child's incomplete thoughts, pauses, and long-winded examples do not bother the child listener. Their empathy at this age is unique, as children recognize each other's efforts to communicate important thoughts.

Tim plucked out his writing journal from the early weeks of first grade. He then thumbed through his portfolio, telling us he needed to find something he had just finished the other day. He held out both pieces of writing—one in each fist—to the upturned faces of the first graders and simply said, "*See?*" One of those long silences that are more bothersome to adults than children ensued. Sensing a magical moment, his teacher asked Tim what he wanted the first graders to see. "Well," he said, "there are more words on this page. I use upper and lower case letters here." And as if just then realizing the difference between his first grade and second grade writing he simply added, thrusting one fist forward and then the other for emphasis, "This is words; but *this* is a story."

Tim's comment allowed all of us to share his insight about his own writing. At eight, he already knew the significance of collecting work over time and organizing his thoughts about his own growth. Tim's being able to differentiate between words on a page and "a story" cannot be assigned a number or letter grade. It is what Patricia Carini, former director of Prospect Center in North Bennington, Vermont, refers to as "that in learning which is immeasurable" (Carini, in press).

In that first grade classroom Tim taught all of us how the portfolio acts as a vehicle for connecting prior and present learning. He affirmed for us what we were just hypothesizing, that is, that children can be competent participants in the assessment of their own learning. Our challenge was to bring powerful qualitative anecdotes such as Tim's to a level of value as exemplars of a child's self-evaluation process at work. His wisdom exceeded any intended purpose for portfolios as yet stated by his teachers—or any of us, for that matter. We had not yet envisioned the palpable strength of the child's voice as beautifully articulated by this young student.

We also witnessed the effect of Tim's powerful lesson on the faces of the younger students. As if another traveler had prepared them for the next destination on their long journey, these first graders were genuinely interested and grateful for this preview of second grade. Portfolios reinforce the genuine value of children's talking to other children about these common learning experiences.

Children recognize the benchmarks of learning that make sense to them. The difference between the achievement of writing a story and writing a list of words is so clear that it connects children to a purpose for writing. Hearing this connection stated by another child deepens that understanding. This recognition of learning milestones is encouraged and supported when children are given the opportunity to examine self-selected samples of their work gathered over time. Affirmation of these milestones occurs, however, when children talk to children.

We recognize that our first graders also have wisdom to impart. At our school, in the last few weeks of May, Kindergarten children visit the first grade classrooms. The purpose of this ritual is to give our youngest students an opportunity to speak directly with first graders about that experience. They want to know what first grade is all about. As a Kindergartner's hand is raised to ask a question, the first graders are ready to give an expert's response to these younger students' inquiries.

KINDERGARTNER: Do you tell time in first grade?

FIRST GRADER: Yes, we do.

And with that confident response, the other first graders nodded softly in agreement. A benchmark has been stated.

Making Thinking Seen

Children's awareness of benchmarks of their learning is central to the concept of portfolio and can be facilitated in conversation with the teacher. Knowing which tasks are difficult and which tasks are easy gives a child valuable information toward self-understanding as a learner. Teasing out small steps of learning and assessing performance on each one makes school manageable for the child. One useful tool to assist this reflective interaction is what we refer to as an "easy/hard questionnaire." It's a tool that can be adjusted for the age-specific needs of the child and teacher. The idea is for the teacher to develop a list of tasks and for the child to consider whether these tasks are easy or hard to complete.

TASK   easy ——————————————————————— hard

Easy/Hard Questionnaire Continuum

The tasks listed (see p. 6) cover a wide range of skills and challenges that the child would encounter either in school or outside of school. The questionnaire is best used with an individual child but can be adjusted for group administration. Asking the child to assist you by pilot testing a new questionnaire is one way to introduce this activity. "I'm trying to see whether this questionnaire is a good way to find out what's easy and what's hard for boys and girls. . . . Could you help me?"

Covering all but the first question, you explain the task: "Each question or task has a line next to it. The beginning of the line says 'easy' and the end of the line says 'hard.' Let's read the task together and I'll move the pencil along this line from easy to hard. You tell me when to stop when I've come to the point that tells how easy or hard you think that task is. Then I'll make a dot there."

It's helpful to begin with a task that will clarify whether the child understands the task of the questionnaire. An item like "climbing a mountain" is usually a sure way of getting a dot at the hard end of the continuum. (Although recently an eight-year-old boy asked, "How high is the mountain?" before responding.) The second task is aimed at the easy end of the continuum, again, just to assess whether the child understands how the questionnaire is organized. You may want to hand over the pencil once the child shows understanding of the task.

The easy/hard dichotomy is only one of many that may be used. Instead of easy/hard, the labels of the continuum can be changed to address different questions, for example, "need help/don't need help"; "don't know/know"; "don't understand/understand"; "like/don't like"; "I know/I'm learning"; and so on. This tool is enormously flexible and can be adjusted to assist children and their teachers in developing insights into their learning.

Discovering a Purpose for Portfolios

Why should students assess themselves? What purpose is served by a child telling the story of personal learning? All schools recognize their responsibility to prepare children to assume an active and constructive role in the society of their future. To that end, it makes good sense to engage children in understanding themselves as learners as soon as possible. Establishing a school climate of independence balanced with responsibility is a purposeful objective to which most schools aspire. However, unless this lofty goal is made concrete with tasks and projects that can be recognized by children as real to them, it will remain an abstract ideal that will be difficult to achieve.

Tim's story occurred years after our faculty first decided to explore student portfolios. This very special vignette crystallized for us the significance of our many conversations, readings, and direct experiences with portfolios. Our learning was shaped by these conversations and experiences and, as a result, we were equipped to shape the learning of our students.

Before we were able to *teach* portfolio, we needed to *learn* portfolio. It was the late 1980s when we began working with student portfolios. Our initial common understanding was the same as that

Climbing a mountain	easy ————————————————	hard
Picking up a ball	easy ————————————————	hard
Getting up in the morning	easy ————————————————	hard
Getting ready for school	easy ————————————————	hard
Being on time for the bus	easy ————————————————	hard
Finding your locker	easy ————————————————	hard
Listening to morning meeting on the rug	easy ————————————————	hard
Writing in your journal	easy ————————————————	hard
Working in your math book	easy ————————————————	hard
Passing out the snack	easy ————————————————	hard
Choosing what to do at recess	easy ————————————————	hard
Making friends	easy ————————————————	hard
Reading	easy ————————————————	hard
Asking for help	easy ————————————————	hard
Going home	easy ————————————————	hard

Sample Easy/Hard Questionnaire

of teachers all over the country who were thinking about port-folios—that portfolios might counterbalance the oversimplified in-formation gleaned from test scores. We, too, surmised that concrete examples of students' abilities as expressed through selections of cur-ricular evidence could substantiate the presence of skills or knowl-edge not evidenced by test scores. At first, we even imagined that portfolios might prove test scores wrong!

We supported this purposeful focus for portfolios at first, but were watchful for other benefits as well. Some teachers expressed skepti-cism with the notion of the inadequacies of test scores as the driving agenda behind portfolios. Test scores are really an adult issue. Results of standardized measures provide teachers with information about the strengths and weaknesses of the curriculum. In addition, these standardized measures serve as a primary vehicle of accountability to parents and the community. Test scores tell adults how the school is performing. Our students weren't interested in test scores, but they were very interested in portfolios. With only a few months of port-folio experience we were already sensing there was something more to portfolios than we first imagined. The "something more" was that children cared about them.

Our ability to recognize a natural connection between portfolios and children was, in part, shaped by our districtwide child-centered philosophy (presented in full in the Appendix). Drawing on the roots of the progressive education movement of the early twentieth century, we believe that children benefit from rich, open-ended experiences that require personal involvement and provide opportunities for self-constructed meaning. Our many faculty discussions about children's multiple intelligences also influenced our thinking. How best could we attribute importance to these ways of knowing with our newly de-signed parent reporting format? Our conversations were invaluable as we began to consolidate our thinking about the place of portfolios in a child's learning. All these influences urged us to be mindful of the competence of children and their ability to make meaning out of their learning experiences.

As a result of these initial conversations and our beginning experiences with children organizing their portfolios, we were able to recognize a more substantive rationale for student portfolios beyond proving test scores wrong. We saw portfolios as a tool for children to learn how to tell their unique story of learning. By collecting and reflecting upon samples of their own work, students could gain insight into their own abilities and interests. Portfolios could be a vehicle for children to inject meaning into their own learning experiences.

This crucial shift in our thinking had enormous implications for how we conceptualized the ownership and contents of the portfolio. If we had believed that portfolios should be designed to address the shortcomings of standardized tests, the selections of work would logically correspond to a child's individual test profile. The contents of these portfolios would be carefully selected to respond to (and hopefully dispel) the specific incongruities of standardized measures for each child. A well-written story that included correct punctuation and spelling might counterbalance a low score on a language mechanics sub-test. Successful weekly math quizzes could highlight a child's ability to learn productively in class in contrast to a time-limited test situation. The point is that we would be choosing what to put in the portfolio because refuting a standardized test clearly dictated it.

By lifting the restriction that portfolios needed to be linked to the limitations of standardized ways of assessing student learning, we found a new purpose for portfolios. However, at the same time, we realized we were headed for a lot of discussion, work, and inventive thinking. New issues emerged. Who would be in charge of the portfolio? What would its contents be? Who would decide? Issues of ownership and content became less clear. If portfolios were a tool for children to learn how to tell their own story of learning, who or what would guide its creation? At this point, we had more questions than answers.

Portfolios take time. Conceptualizing the specifics of organization and structure are not tasks that can be accomplished overnight.

Slowly, we came to understand that the only real impediments to creating a new vision of assessment were our own doubts and the time required to cope with resistance to change. We didn't hurry—we didn't superimpose unrelated agendas on our work—we did it the right way. The following chapters tell the story.

Reflection Tag

I chose this piece for my portfolio because . . .

It's important to remember that children think about learning in different ways than their teachers. Multiple Intelligences theory served as our passageway to portfolios. The idea that children learn all the time made good sense to us. It caused us to take a critical look at our teaching and assessment practices.

LESSON 2

Children Learn All the Time

Sam, Eric, and Jimmy enter the block corner in their first grade classroom. Wearing big, unlaced sneakers, each boy tiptoes through the miniature construction site, carefully figuring out how to reach favorite blocks without disturbing the structures already completed by other children.

Jimmy asks Eric, "Are you part of our building team?" signaling to him that perhaps the other two are already a team. "I can attach this bridge over here," Eric responds with confidence. He is now accepted into the crew. Scratching his neck and putting one hand on his hip Jimmy asks, "What can we build?" He looks to the other two to see how his question is received.

"Guys, I'm making a huge trampoline," announces Sam. "What's that word you used?" asks Jimmy with great interest. "You know, you jump on it and go high," says Sam. "Oh yeah . . . I know that . . . let's make it really big." Jimmy, Sam, and Eric are now working on the trampoline. They assess what blocks are needed, retrieve them, and pass them to each other to place on the tower of blocks. "Can you come to my house after school?" Sam asks Jimmy.

The lights go off. A child's voice announces the end of choice time. "Time to clean up!" With her finger still on the light switch she speaks with the authority of a teacher. She is the "clean-up announcer" this week. Her classmates accord her the respect deserved by that important job. The boys end their play and begin to put the room back in order.

Returning to the writing table Jimmy begins to record the important happenings of that morning in his journal. In first grade invented spelling he prints these sentences: "We made a trampoline with blocks. You can jump on it and go high. I'm going to Sam's house after school." A new word is learned, a new friendship made. What a great day!

Children recognize a broader range of valued abilities, and attribute importance to them more evenly, than do their teachers. Children observe each other carefully and they are aware of what each does well. Knowing big words, having great ideas for the block corner, making a good "clean-up" announcement, being a good friend, are all highly acknowledged qualifications for life in the mind of a first grader. Observing these accomplishments in each other is how children make sense of their social world. Young children link such perceptions in ways that create meaning in their lives.

As an institution the school begins to place a higher priority on some competencies than others. Knowing big words comes to matter more, officially, than having great ideas for the block corner. Schools have to do this. As an extension of the culture in which they exist, schools communicate a hierarchy of skills that reinforces the stated values and goals of their culture. The school's apportionment of value connected to varying competencies is different from the child's. But isn't the child's intuitive sense of valuable knowledge another important dimension of learning? The ability to form friendships, to use materials creatively, to speak with authority, are in fact reliable predictors of success and usefulness in society. Given that, schools need to authenticate those values so clearly communicated in the block corner and recognize their viability.

Furthermore, by acknowledging and affirming a more inclusive spectrum of children's abilities, schools could convey the fullness and variety of what matters to children and thereby increase the likelihood that all children would become more confident learners. Viewing the job of learning from the child's perspective is not easily done, but at our school we have learned that portfolios can be a vehicle to achieve this goal.

Children Know in Multiple Ways
But We Value Only Some of Them

I was a new principal—anxious for innovation that would define my role but also anxious to show that I respected how these teachers, new to me but not to each other, communicated what really mattered to them. As many new principals are known to do, I developed that habit of loading mailboxes with professional articles in search of a stimulus for good collegial conversation. The response to an article about Howard Gardner's theory of multiple intelligences (Gardner, 1983) indicated both interest and a desire for further information. A few months later, many of us were able to attend a lecture by Dr. Gardner when he visited a neighboring community. We liked what we heard and we brought these new insights back to school with us to mull over with the rest of the staff.

Our discussions about children's multiple intelligences served as our passageway to student portfolios—but not right away. Before we were able to gather evidence of our students' knowledge, we needed to recognize the many faces of learning. Gardner's well-known theory asserts that there are at least seven different kinds of intelligences: Musical, Linguistic, Logical-Mathematical, Spatial, Bodily-Kinesthetic, Interpersonal, and Intrapersonal. (He notes possible additional intelligences—Naturalist and Spiritual or Existential—in *Intelligence Reframed*, 1999, p. 66.) The main thrust of Gardner's theory as applied to schools is that children may demonstrate these intelligences in ways that are not necessarily associated with traditional school subjects and (of more relevance to our future work with portfolios) not examined by traditional assessment tools.

We were intrigued by this simple and yet compelling model for understanding how and where children learn. It served to remind us of what we wanted our teaching to reinforce. Recognizing children's different learning abilities resonated with our own beliefs of how children learn. The idea of attributing importance to children's intelligences as demonstrated in all phases of their lives seemed so very useful in explaining to parents how their children learn. At first, we envisioned that this perspective would supplement the limited information gleaned from standardized tests. In addition, the multiple intelligences overview was an opportunity for us to recommit ourselves to our district's accepted belief in the uniqueness of each child's way of learning.

At that time, we were a faculty of diverse ages, interests, and experience. Nevertheless, we all embraced an explanation that caused us to reconsider our notions of learning. At some level, all of us connected personally to this theory. We recalled our own early school experiences, when our own multiple intelligences went unnoticed and unappreciated by our teachers. We recognized that what captured the youthful imagination was often not acknowledged or valued. Our teachers, among the most powerful and cherished people in our lives, could have encouraged us to pursue what really mattered to us. But for many of us the opportunity was lost simply because most teachers didn't know how to fit our passions into their curriculum.

Now we were the teachers. Our personal bond to these ideas of *many ways of knowing* and *encouraging children's passions* proved to be the most powerful source of the energy we needed to embed its truths into our daily teaching practice.

The connection between our own experiences as childhood learners and our sincere wish to compensate for the omissions of our former teachers gave us an implicit rationale to explore what really mattered to our students. But how would we attribute importance to *all* of these intelligences?—especially those intelligences not directly observable in the academic classroom? How could we abandon ingrained ways of viewing the curriculum as a hierarchy, and find ways to acknowledge a child's successes in solving a mathematical equation as on a par with successes in composing a musical phrase or maintaining physical balance on the beam? Was some learning more valuable than other learning? How would we report children's learning to parents, and would they accept a more even attribution of importance to all areas of the curriculum? These were the large open-ended questions we discussed in those early years. None of us entered this conversation without prior experience as both a student and a teacher. We began to realize that visceral beliefs about learning become part of who we are and cannot easily be set aside.

Unlearning is far more difficult than learning, but a confluence of factors and, most important, lucky timing resulted in all of us being able to unlearn together. Being a new principal gave me a chance to start fresh. The whole staff shared feelings of uneasiness about the rising importance of standardized tests and a desire to reaffirm our commitment to a broader concept of learning. We wanted to have that commitment legitimized by a larger public. A growing faculty searching for common ground and inspiration, we were ripe for the influences of a large idea that could focus our efforts.

Where Does Learning Take Place?

Does learning take place only during reading, writing, and math lessons in the classroom? Certainly not. Just ask any teacher and you will hear countless stories of students learning in the art studio, in the gymnasium, on the playground, at scouts, or while baby-sitting. Yet most schools still have an implicitly hierarchical notion of curriculum. The language arts, math, science, and social studies are "more important" than the so-called noncore or special subjects of art, music, physical education, second language, and technology.

Schools organize the day and allot time and space in ways that relegate special subjects and their teachers to a secondary role. Although they do know the special subjects are equally valuable to children, teachers may set this knowledge aside and compete for instructional minutes in support of specific curricula and programs as well as adequate preparation time during the instructional day.

Although our goal is to help the child make meaningful connections between disparate experiences, we sometimes organize the school day in a way that makes it unlikely.

Understandably we each view our particular program or our subject as the most important feature of a child's education. We do know that every teacher's contribution is only a portion of a child's larger learning journey. However, we tend to see the parts and not the whole. Recognizing how our subject or program fits into the child's learning is a task for all teachers to address. Anticipating the interconnections to larger goals is necessary if those connections are really going to be made. It shouldn't be left entirely to the child to assemble all the separate pieces of learning into a meaningful whole.

Gardner's theory of multiple intelligences was a sturdy scaffolding for us to organize and consolidate our thinking about the value of children's curricular experiences. We didn't seize upon this expanded notion of children's learning as the final answer to how to assess children's learning. Rather, we kept Gardner's theory close by in that fuzzy world of inspiration. This concept flowed naturally into the course of our daily teaching. We resisted the temptation to organize our instructional program around the well-defined "seven intelligences" because we recognized that these designations were the author's arbitrary examples of a much larger idea, that is, that children's learning takes place all the time.

We began to make use of Gardner's theory when we talked to parents about their children's learning and also when we wrote evaluative reports. We made deliberate efforts to note "instances of children's intelligences" that lay outside the more traditional subjects of reading, writing, math, science, and social studies. And we were especially attentive to students who were less able to demonstrate strengths in school subjects but clearly had considerable intelligence in other areas. The question of how to attribute value to learning that takes place outside of our classrooms is an enormous task for teachers to grapple with. We found we needed more concrete examples to give definitional boundaries to our many notions.

Connecting the Theory to Our Experience

Jeff was in fourth grade at just that time when we were trying so hard to incorporate Gardner's ideas into our observations. School was not easy for Jeff. Teachers were perplexed about how best to help him. He continued to lag behind his peers in most school subjects. But in one of many conversations with his teacher, Jeff noted that he played golf rather well and, in fact, was going to be in a local competition the following weekend. Perhaps buoyed by recent faculty conversations about multiple intelligences or just acting on her own excellent intuition, Jeff's teacher encouraged him to bring in a videotape of his golf tournament debut for her to watch. She subsequently shared the tape with me.

After viewing Jeff's videotape, I sensed a teachable moment for our faculty, and so I asked Jeff if I could share the videotape with all the teachers in a meeting. As if enjoying his fame, he smiled and agreed. Little did he know that he would become our best example of multiple intelligences within the confines of our faculty room. We set up two video monitors side by side. I popped the video of Jeff's golf tournament into one monitor. On the other was a video of classroom footage that included Jeff involved in discussion and transition to a math lesson. We turned down the sound and silently observed the face of this youngster as it appeared on both screens. On the left screen we observed the confident and intent expression of Jeff as he demonstrated a high degree of competence, reading the green in preparation for his putt. The success and attendant good feelings associated with acknowledged ability were undeniably evident. On the right screen we witnessed a very different image—a boy unsure of what materials should be on his desk and unable to follow the focused exchange of the class discussion. Jeff had little of the control he showed in his golf game. Clearly, Jeff was far less successful with the learning agenda of school subjects.

As we watched the video screens we were all cheering for Jeff as teachers do, both in support of any child involved in a successful venture and in recognition and remembrance of our own school days. We could easily relate to stories of successful learning in nonschool environments. The dual images of Jeff helped us to make sense of multiple views of a child's learning and to uncover our deeply ingrained habits of focusing on in-classroom learning as superior to any other kind of learning.

Jeff's videotape sparked a creative explosion in the faculty room that day. The puzzled sighs that usually accompanied conversations about Jeff were transformed into animated exchanges about how to attribute value to Jeff's successful learning and, recognizing this talent, how to bring these feelings of competence into his school world.

When teachers gather to focus on a child's needs there is no limit to the possibility of positive outcomes. The exchange of ideas and strategies based on years of teaching experience coupled with a love of the task is a pleasure to witness. We were unwittingly and metaphorically rummaging around in our own memory boxes in the faculty room that day. And we were compensating for those omissions of our former teachers who were not unwilling but just unable to understand our learning in a way that acknowledged our different talents and our passions.

We reviewed Jeff's current levels of performance in the classroom and noted that although he struggled with the vocabulary and the ideas present in the novel that his class was reading, he had expert knowledge of the concepts and strategies of golf. His ability to write about his golf skills was limited, so we hesitated to ask Jeff to report them to his classmates and risk the embarrassment associated with his academic deficits. The idea of making a "big book" about golf for our first graders was put forth and immediately gained momentum. Organized by his teacher and one of our PTA volunteers, Jeff carefully laid out the design of a book that identified the attire, equipment, and strategies of the golfer in simple language and pictures. After the book was laminated, Jeff went on tour to each first grade classroom to present the book and review its contents. The extra added attraction of Jeff's taking them outside for a demonstration of the game of golf delighted these young students, who discovered a new hero in their midst.

Jeff was also affected by this collective focus on his learning. He was acknowledged by his peers, his teachers, and his principal for his hard-earned skill. His self-confidence was bolstered. In the following months of his final elementary school year we noticed that Jeff was beginning to transfer some of the focus and energy obviously present in his golf game to the more difficult tasks for him of learning school subjects.

Our next collective task as a faculty was to symbolically visualize that other video monitor for all our students. We had to have the image of each face—happy, eager, alert, confident—before us. This task is not as easy as it sounds. To recognize that children have learning lives outside our classrooms is obvious, but it is not deliberately articulated in the school. With new purpose, we began to share the many stories of our students' successes on stage at the community theater, at the ice rink, at the podium for the student council elections, on the playground comforting a friend, on the school bus assisting a substitute driver, in the art room forming a clay sculpture, in the auditorium moving to the sounds of a musical performance. No longer were these vignettes shared simply as stories of our students' lives outside of real learning. We began to attribute importance to these stories as connected events in the learning history of each child.

Teachers are among the heroes and heroines of our lives. The acknowledgment and approval that a child receives from a teacher can have significant and long-term positive effects in bolstering the energy required to approach more difficult projects. The risk-taking behavior that every learner engages in can be effectively counterbalanced by mutual understanding and support for successful experiences, even if they have not occurred in the school setting. Detecting and supporting the passions of students, especially those that exist outside the school setting, is what memorable teachers do to support the multiple ways in which children learn best.

But how can we showcase each child in ways that would encourage development as a confident learner? How can we even begin to know what talents and competencies our students may have that are not part of our school's curriculum? The first step is to recognize that we can't always know and so we need to create a school climate where all of children's different ways of learning are honored. The second step is to spend time, as a class and as a faculty, talking about different ways of knowing.

Jeff's story was the genuine example we were looking for that allowed us to move forward. At a time when the national media focused on publishing results of standardized tests and portraying schools as deficient, we felt we were rediscovering what really mattered about children. We felt we had the energy and the will to find a way to counterbalance those negative stereotypic stories about schools. We began to think how to teach parents to view their child's learning in this expanded manner. We decided to redesign our parent conference reporting form so that all of us would be communicating a comparable message about each child's multiple learning opportunities.

Transferring all these conversations and insights into a visual format was our next goal. Redesigning our parent reporting form proved to be an invaluable project because it consolidated our thinking about how to attribute importance to children's diverse learning experiences. We were beginning to construct our collective portfolio.

Reflection Tag

I chose this piece for my portfolio because . . .

It reminds me of the importance of teachers' talking to teachers and forming personal and professional bonds. Teachers need a supportive and stimulating school environment if they are to create these same conditions for their students. Looking at our own habits and preconceptions can create negative feelings—unless the community of the school offers support and encouragement. Luckily for us, we were able to take that big step.

LESSON 3

Teachers Learn All the Time, Too

We gathered in the faculty room to design the form that would serve as a public symbol of our collective revolution. Brimming with a sense of being enlightened, eager to serve as advocates for children's ways of learning, and wanting to set ourselves apart a bit from the other schools in our small district, we set about our work. We envisioned our new reporting form as a unique statement in support of the multifaceted nature of children's learning. Our new recognition of children's ability to participate in the assessment of their own learning was an energizing idea to pursue. Our revolution went unnoticed by anyone other than we who were in that faculty room, but nonetheless, it was a significant event in our school's history.

Only in retrospect can I appreciate the importance of our many conversations about the revision of our parent reporting form. What would normally be a routine task became, for us, a breakthrough event. As Tim had, we too were beginning to differentiate between our words and "a story." We wanted to look beyond the words of our teacher-written evaluations of students to tell the real story of each child's learning. Redesigning how we reported children's learning to parents caused us to reconsider our notion of curriculum and our unexamined attitudes about what mattered in education. This was a crucial step toward our yet–to-be-imagined exploration of student portfolios. Most important, however, this project brought children closer to the heart of the assessment process.

Designing a New Reporting Form
Activates an Innovative Spirit

Our school district has a long tradition of acknowledging the uniqueness of each child's learning. A significant feature of our school district's history and progressive philosophy is the absence of letter grades in the elementary schools. Our purpose is to recognize the complexity of learning best described in a conversation with parents and student rather than a single letter grade. For many years, we have reported elementary students' progress to parents through conferences supported by written notations. The headings of the reporting form guided teachers in their reflections upon each child's growth. These organizing headings were Language Arts, Math, Science, Social Studies, Growth of the Child as a Learner, and Growth of the Child as a Group Member. These broad guidelines for assessing student progress had been suggested by one of the many districtwide faculty committees and study groups that have come to define the outstanding professional culture that exists in the Winnetka Public Schools.

Stimulated by our recent discussions of multiple intelligences theory, Crow Island School teachers decided to take a closer look at our districtwide reporting form, which now seemed insufficient to express the idea that learning takes place all the time. We began to note that nowhere did the form direct us to think about reporting to parents about a child's successes or stage of development in Art, Music, Physical Education, Spanish, Library, and Technology—all part of our comprehensive curriculum.

We began to think about the possibilities of a new reporting format that would add a visual image for our new insights. In a very primitive way, we put the stick figure of a child in the center of an overhead slide and drew projecting circles to surround the figure. We called our first rough attempt the "floating circles."

This primitive drawing was a beginning image for us that captured the idea of the multiple dimensions of a child's learning. We avoided placing the seven multiple intelligences in these floating circles. Gardner's theory served us best as an inspiration, not a template.

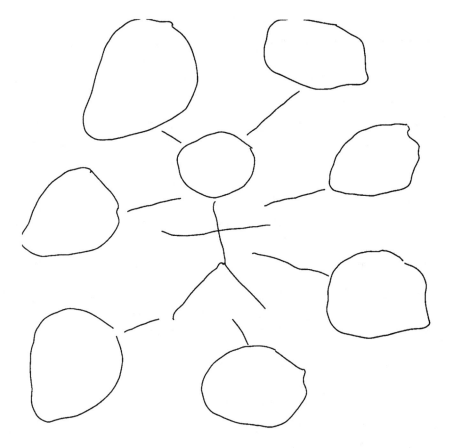

Floating Circles

We began to think about which subjects or learning areas we would note in these circles and how we would describe them. In support of a multiple intelligences perspective, we were looking for more inclusive terminology that attributed equal value to the diversity of children's learning opportunities.

Attempting to unlearn our habit of thinking in terms of the subject areas, we began to use the descriptor "learning experiences" to refer to the many diverse aspects of a child's learning. New language signals new thinking. The coining of this term was another sign that we were beginning to shift our thinking from traditional ways of viewing learning to a more comprehensive and multi-dimensional model.

Trying to think about children's learning as separate from our teaching required us to rid ourselves of ingrained assumptions about curriculum and evaluation. We needed to extend our old concept of valued learning to include how a child creates an appropriate accompaniment to a song, what decisions a child makes about color and media to complete a collage, which strategies a child uses to ensure that a soccer ball reaches its intended destination, and a child's experience of figuring out how to settle a dispute fairly on the playground.

At the same time that we were stretching our minds to accommodate this monumental revision in our thinking we were also focused on the many details and specifics of the design of the actual form. We soon learned that transferring ideas into visual images is not an easy task. The visual thinkers on our faculty took the lead here.

Activating Our Own Multiple Intelligences: Opportunities for Staff Development

Reflecting on those crucial discussions, I now recognize that what helped to move us along was the chance for all of us to display our own multiple intelligences. In discussions about curriculum we often talk about providing large curricular concepts for children that offer many entries into a topic. Unfortunately, we don't always recognize our need for that same curricular model for our own growth. It's called good staff development.

The revolutionary climate that surrounded our project emanated from the shared commitment that we all felt. No matter what our interests or talents, there was a need for what we had to offer. We had to work out the philosophical issues that would define our purposes. We needed to confront the political implications of our project, that is, how would parents react to this new format? We had to create a single visual format that would capture all our ideas. We also wanted to consider how the child's voice could be included in this process.

The visual thinkers were the first to create a product. Those faculty members who wished to contribute their energies toward the particulars of the design of the form met and presented their suggestions to the rest. This group took our initial primitive stick figure and circle design and transformed it into a usable graphic. Conversations at these faculty meetings refined our original floating circles format and yielded an 11"x17" sheet with open rectangular spaces and a circle in the center. We called it our Learning Experiences Form.

New Ideas Stimulate Courage . . . and Doubts as Well

I remember the day the printer delivered the boxes of our newly printed Learning Experiences Forms. Teachers happily noted their arrival in the office on their way to their mailboxes. Somehow the printer's identifying label on the outside of the box—"Learning Experiences"—buoyed our enthusiasm once again. It was as if the printer's label had legitimized our new terminology.

But the good feelings associated with the successful completion of the first stage of our project began to dissipate. As we examined our newly imagined document we realized, as if for the first time, that it was in fact a large, empty sheet of paper with rectangles and a circle on it. The open-endedness of our new form was both exhilarating and stressful. The idea that one teacher's form might look different from another's caused some of us to retreat a bit and find safety in those familiar and traditional organizers of the academic subject areas. The concern that parents might not accept these forms if they weren't all the same was one way of projecting our own anxiety. The major question that surfaced, albeit quietly, was, "How do we label the tabs?" (that is, what to write on the label section adjacent to each rectangle). We could easily transfer the academic subject organizers of Language Arts, Science, Social Studies, and Math to these labels but that seemed insufficiently innovative in light of our discussions about multiple ways of knowing.

Committed to the multiple intelligences perspective, we decided to include rectangular spaces written by the teachers of Art, Music, Physical Education, Spanish, and Library and Technology. This was a major step toward acknowledging these teachers' long-term relationships with all students, the value of their programs, and their insights

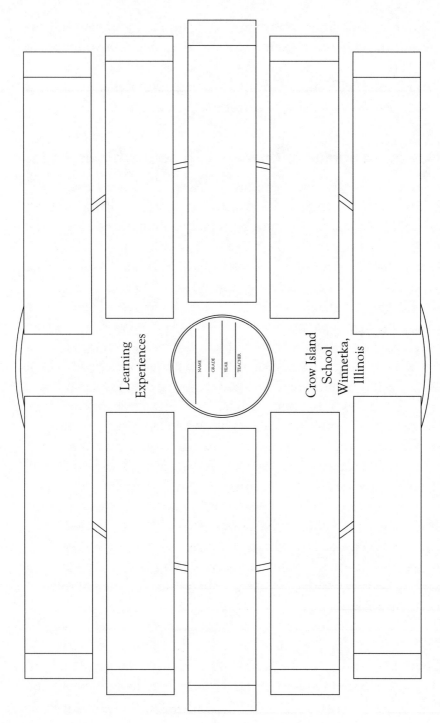

Learning Experiences

NAME
GRADE
YEAR
TEACHER

Crow Island
School
Winnetka,
Illinois

Blank Learning Experiences Form. *Note:* This is a reduction; actual size of form is 11"x17".

about a child's learning. This inclusive way of attributing value to all subjects portrayed instruction as a coordinated and comprehensive program rather than a hierarchical ordering of separate subjects. We would find in future years that this particular issue required further attention, but at the time we were designing our Learning Experiences Form the special subjects were provided with an equal rectangle.

But what about the other tabs? We realized that one of the qualities we appreciated most about each other was that each of us had a uniqueness to our teaching—an interest or emphasis or passion that defined us, at least to each other, as innovators of curriculum and good teachers. But was it OK to talk about this uniqueness? The dialogue was courteous but expressed real anxiety.

Q: How should I label the tabs?

A: That depends on how you organize instruction.

Q: But what if my tabs are different from the ones another teacher at my grade level uses?

A: That's OK. Although curriculum content is a constant, you organize instruction differently. We already know that about each other. Now we're just writing about it.

Q: But we organize instruction differently for different students.

A: Yes, and the Learning Experience Form can and should reflect these differences.

Still new to the principalship, I did not recognize at that time how these questions represented teachers in their naked state. Looking back, it's good that I didn't understand that. Nevertheless, I could appreciate that this was a critical stage in our thinking. The form was bringing to the surface what I term the bilingualism of teachers. Somewhere very early in teachers' careers, we learn how to become fluent in two languages, "inside language" and "outside language."

Inside language is what we actually do in our classrooms. It reflects our beliefs and values, years of teaching experience, observations of children over time—and of other good teachers as well—and good old confidence in knowing what we know. Teachers use inside language to voice uncertainties and to seek a sympathetic and helpful response from a colleague.

Outside language is what we say we do in our classrooms. It is influenced by community values, relative comfort level within the school environment, parental expectations, political pressures, district and administrative policies and procedures, test scores, and the stated curriculum. Teachers use outside language to characterize their teaching as being predominantly effective and to attribute criticisms of their teaching to external influences outside of their control.

We are cautious about speaking inside language and require feelings of safety and security to do so. Our discussions about attributing importance to children's multiple intelligences required us to speak inside and, in so doing, we were gradually able to have the kinds of discussions and sharing of values that can lead to the creation of a secure and thoughtful environment not only for teachers but for children and parents as well.

We soon realized that we couldn't change the ways we evaluate children's learning without taking a close look at ourselves. This process required openness, trust, intimacy, and a great deal of sharing. As we began to delve into the complicated issues of assessing what and how children learn, we found ourselves undergoing an intensive assessment of our teaching, our beliefs about children, and how we view the school and its relationship to the community it serves. At the same time we realized that our proposed Learning Experiences Form would be unique to our school. Although our district has always encouraged initiatives and staff development projects, we weren't entirely certain how this particular project would be accepted by the district and the community.

Changing Our Ways of Reporting Children's Growth

Taking a courageous step forward, we used the new form at the next conference period. In the beginning, some teachers cautiously carried over the old organizers of the previous format onto the new form. Others ventured out and coined new organizing labels that better reflected their style of teaching and the ways they integrated the curriculum. Labels such as Writing/Spelling, Math Computation/Facts, Problem Solving: Math/Science, Activity Time, Peer Relationships, Independence/Use of Materials, Communication Skills, Social/Emotional Development, Class Meeting, and Self-Directed Learning Time indicated that teachers were reconsidering how they organized instruction and what they considered important.

As noted, the special subjects teachers also contributed to each child's form. In those prenetworking days, we devised a system of writing student progress statements on 2"x5" stickers that were given to the classroom teachers to affix to each child's Learning Experience Form. Depending on how each classroom teacher labeled the rectangles, some of these stickers were placed within a rectangle and some were affixed to the top, bottom, or back of the form. All ten rectangles were of equal size, and the "specials stickers" fit into the rectangles. This small but monumental detail served as a visual reminder to all of us that all subjects in a comprehensive instructional program—not just the basics—should carry the same weight and have equal potential to provide learning experiences.

As teachers struggled with the new format in preparation for the conference, they became more thoughtful. Parents sensed the positive energy of this new format and in turn became more aware of the depth and breadth of their child's school experiences. The first parent conference using this form provided immediate positive responses from both parents and teachers.

After using these forms for one or two reporting periods, we shared samples with each other and collected our suggestions for revisions. One unanticipated problem that came to light was that these early reports tended to be more descriptive of the curriculum specifics than the child's learning. As a remedy, one teacher suggested that a grade level's Curriculum Overview be printed onto the back of the form. This overview consisted of brief statements of grade-level curriculum objectives for that portion of the school year. Teachers of

Learning Experiences

Kate Leary
NAME
GRADE 5
YEAR Winter 1992
TEACHER Mrs. Saunders

PASTE PHOTO HERE

Crow Island School
Winnetka, Illinois

Reading

Kate has developed into a wonderful and fluent reader. She derives pleasure from reading and always has one or two novels on her desk. During class discussion she demonstrates an ability to read with understanding, make inferences, predict outcomes, and discuss story structure.

Science

Kate works well in partner and cooperative group activities. She has been enthusiastic about our Energy Unit activities. This year she participated in our Science Invention Fair. Her project, "The Easy Dog Feeder," was creative, well planned, and thoughtfully presented.

Social Studies

In our work with rivers and world geography, Kate has shown quick understanding of the interaction between human and environment. She is adept at gathering information from a variety of maps and shows a good ability to relate these facts to their social consequences.

Work Habits

Kate is an active and interested learner and moves through the day with energy and enthusiasm. Kate enjoys people. She loves to watch the interactions between those around her and she is able to engage in dialogue with classmates on any topic. Kate is developing an understanding of the importance of good work habits.

Writing/Spelling

Kate is an outstanding writer. Kate demonstrates persistence in working with a story, rewriting the plot until she is satisfied with the end result. Her attention to detail and choice of words are excellent. She consistently receives excellent scores on weekly spelling tests and is able to execute these strong skills in her writing.

Art

Kate has developed into a very hard-working young artist throughout this school year. Her ability to focus and concentrate in class has enabled her to produce quality work. Kate seems to enjoy working with all of the mediums and also seems comfortable in expressing her artistic creativity. It has been my pleasure to have Kate in art class.

Math

Kate is justifiably proud of her abilities and achievement in math. She has progressed smoothly through the fifth grade curriculum demonstrating a good understanding and facility with fractions, multiplication, and division. She uses problem-solving strategies efficiently and she is willing to take her time for quality.

Music

Kate has been doing an excellent job in music. She has a good sense of pitch and a strong singing voice. She is enthusiastic about performing and has contributed positively to our last performance project. She is a creative problem-solver and has applied it well in a variety of situations. Kate is a pleasure to have in class.

Personal Growth

Kate has so much enthusiasm. She is truly a positive force in the classroom. She is conscientious about her work and uses her assignment notebook to advantage. She has been learning to work ahead of time to avoid a crunch at the last minute.

Physical Education

Kate is an excellent student in the fifth grade physical education. She shows fine motor skills in all areas with a particular ability in gymnastics. Her classmates voted her to be a team captain in After School Sports volleyball.

Sample Completed Learning Experiences Form. *Note:* This is a reduction; actual size of form is 11"x17".

special subjects would also prepare grade-level descriptive statements and these would be included on the form as well. The addition of this overview freed up the front of the form for more focused description of each child's learning (see sample curriculum overview on pp. 34–35).

We were grateful to our colleague for suggesting we include an overview of the curriculum. It exemplified one of many problem-solving conversations we would have and the generous disposition of this community of teachers. This easy remedy was also a very rich solution in that it created a natural dialogue among teachers at each grade level as they saw the usefulness of creating a single overview. In addition, the special subject curricular content was now in print on the form. Both teachers and parents would be provided with a helpful explanation of the goals and content of the curricular strands of Art, Music, Physical Education, Spanish, and Library and Technology.

A Place for the Child's Voice

Over months and years we refined the form to meet the needs and suggestions of teachers at different grade levels. Teachers became more comfortable in customizing the form to reflect how they organized instruction at Kindergarten, Primary, and Intermediate grade levels. Although the child was figuratively at the center of this form (with name and photo), we began to feel the absence of the child's input, and so we designated one of the spaces for a Child Reflection, which was intended to represent each student's current thoughts about current learning. We devised ways of taking dictation for the younger students and provided large adhesive labels for the older students on which they would record their thoughts about their school year thus far. We would then affix these large labels onto the Learning Experience Form. Soon after, we began to ask parents to share their thoughts about their child's learning and we included their reflections on this Learning Experience Form as well. This Learning Experiences Form was included in each child's cumulative file and served as a formal record of progress similar to a report card.

Sample Curriculum Overview

CURRICULUM OVERVIEW
Fall—Second Grade

LANGUAGE ARTS: During Writing Workshop, children choose topics and genre. They work through the process of planning, writing, revising, editing, and publishing. During Reading Workshop, children read a variety of literature with focus on sight word development, word identification skills, reading fluency, comprehension strategies, and enhancement of prior knowledge. Other activities include spelling lessons, phonics activities, handwriting exercises, word games, and independent reading. Resources include anthologies of literature, trade books, published writing from children in the class, and spelling workbooks.

MATH: The Winnetka Public Schools second grade math curriculum includes the following content strands: patterns and relationships; number sense and numeration; whole number operations; measurement, geometry, and spatial sense; and making sense of data. Special emphasis is placed on practicing the basic addition and subtraction facts. Resources include *Second Grade Everyday Mathematics*, developed by the University of Chicago School Mathematics Project, and the Winnetka math workbooks and games.

SCIENCE: *SCIIS 3* Interactions and Systems and Life Cycles provide the basic foundation for the physical and life science sequences. The primary focus in the fall is on Interactions and Systems. Children will examine chemical systems and electrical circuits to observe and interpret evidence on interaction. They will make predictions, collect and chart data, and write individual journals and lab reports.

SOCIAL STUDIES: The concept of community is developed throughout the year. We start by focusing on our classroom; our daily meetings and weekly "Star of the Week" program help build a sense of community. We also learn about the community of Winnetka, including its history and services. The Location Book provides children with opportunities to explore their place in the geographical world around them. We study Crow Island School, Lake Michigan, Illinois, the United States of America, North America, Earth, and the solar system. Activities include map skills, development of geography vocabulary, and field trips.

Sample Curriculum Overview, *continued*

SOCIAL DEVELOPMENT: Throughout a given day, the class collaborates as a whole, in small groups, and in partnerships. These groupings help to develop new bonds and respect for diversity. The children are expected to develop resourcefulness and to assume increased responsibility. Independent activities (Activity Time) allow the children to construct their own agenda and to interact within classroom expectations. Emphasis is on cooperation, collaboration, problem solving, and decision making. Choices include writing, reading, dramatics, block building, art center, board games, math games, and computer.

ART: We have started an exciting year of experiencing a variety of materials, tools, and techniques. In second grade art, we strengthen manipulative skills, stress original thinking, and develop appreciation of our own work, the work of our classmates, and the work of professional artists.

MUSIC: The focus of second grade music has been on experiencing the basic elements of music sound. Building on their experiences in first grade music classes, students have been exploring steady beats, faster and slower tempos, duple and triple meter, notes of longer and shorter duration, melodic contour, and basic musical forms. We have begun to use visual symbols to represent music sounds and have been developing good use of our singing voices.

PHYSICAL EDUCATION: Second graders are learning to shift from the "I/We" orientation of first grade to a "We/Us" focus through the team concept in participation. Children are developing team loyalties and strategies by involvement in relays, games of low organization, and activities of increased complexity such as kick ball, Crow Island field hockey, blam-ball, and two-ball soccer.

RESOURCE CENTER: Students will listen to stories, videos, filmstrips, and tapes; use computer programs; learn library arrangement; select books for pleasure and assignments; and learn to use the reading lofts and library appropriately.

SPANISH: Primary goals for second grade are increasing capacity to listen for longer periods of time and answering questions with one- or two-word answers. Beginning reading consists of memorizing pattern books through repetition. The thematic unit for the year centers on the Guatemalan or Peruvian culture.

Here are some sample reflections:

I think I've grown from a child in this class to a student. I've looked at my portfolio at the beginning of the year and found that I have grown. Going to this school I will learn a great deal. I really love it here. I've changed from not knowing my math facts and division to knowing them both. I've tried hard and it's starting to pay off.

—Sally, fourth grade

Sally is a conceptual thinker. She has a great imagination and she is enjoying school. We hope there will be opportunities for her to enhance her creative abilities and to feel confident about her abilities and talents.

—Sally's parents

The designation of space for children's reflections within the Learning Experiences Form spurred our thinking toward the idea of portfolios. We were pleased with how readily our students shared their thoughts about their accomplishments and the challenges of school. It occurred to us that it would make sense for children to connect these thoughts with specific pieces of their schoolwork. We didn't have a clear idea of how to implement this notion, but we wanted time to think through the possibilities. Now we were in the act of discovering portfolios for ourselves.

Reflection Tag

I chose this piece for my portfolio because . . .

We were overly focused on the content of the portfolio, not realizing that ownership and purpose are really the key issues. The interrelationship of these three elements is an evolving process worked out by teacher and child over time. Surprisingly this process is not at all confusing for students . . . they understand it better than we do.

LESSON 4

Getting Clear on Portfolio Purpose, Ownership, and Content

We began to gather evidence of children's learning. Each teacher intuited how best to approach the task of selecting samples for these rudimentary portfolios. Our awareness of our own role in this task was still a work in progress. My role as principal was to listen, observe, and support the evolving spirit of innovation and exploration.

First Steps

Realizing we needed firsthand experience with the task of compiling portfolios, we immersed ourselves in the concreteness of the collecting activity. Most of us gathered a sampling of children's work across all curricular areas. Writing captured our immediate attention, as a child's growth is most easily observed by the juxtaposition of early and later samples. We added completed math workbooks and spelling tests, social studies reports, lists of books read by the child, and science lab reports. These initial portfolios were a blend of process and product.

In those early years, we used large computer boxes for storage. Individual files were made of folded sheets of art paper. Later, hanging file folders became a popular organizing tool. The issue of what work was sent home and what work stayed in the classroom was important in the early years. It took time to help the parents realize that the majority of children's work would stay at school.

The collections became unwieldy almost at once. Many hours of faculty and class discussion were spent on the details of the type and color of containers, the location and labeling of the intermediate gathering folders, the importance of dating all student work, and our directions to the children about what to select. A teacher subcommittee suggested we color-code the grade-level portfolios. Each child's portfolio (that is, single-year collection of work) would be contained in a 9.5"x14.5" accordion file. Those for the first grade would be red, second grade, yellow, third grade, blue, and fourth grade, green. Fifth grade teachers, expressing the need for a different organizing tool, decided to use large-ringed black binders with subject organizers. The Kindergarten teachers, after years of experimentation with a variety of booklets and containers that could include larger pieces of work, decided on manila file folders.

Because we wanted to keep these collections together throughout the student's six elementary years at Crow Island, we selected a 10"x15" red-roped expandable envelope that could potentially hold all five grade-level (K–4) folders. The fifth grade black binder remained separate. We called this larger envelope an archive. We affixed white file labels in the upper left corner of the larger archival envelope and entered each student's name, last name first for alphabetizing.

As we became comfortable with the physical aspects of the portfolio, we returned to our earlier conversations about the child's involvement. The notion that children could and should participate was intriguing to us but how would it work? How would the child know what to choose? What if a child didn't select balanced evidence of the curriculum for the portfolio? Should all portfolios have the same content? Would it be appropriate for a child to present a portfolio that excluded a major content area? These questions signaled that we were grappling with the thorny issues of purpose and ownership.

We tried out different ideas. We designed portfolio tasks for students that would give them some experience with each stage of the portfolio process—stages we were just learning ourselves. Teachers directed the children to gather examples of their own writing over the course of the year. To give students an intermediate gathering folder for their work many teachers had sets of hanging file folders for different subjects. Writing, Math, and Other filing bins were set out in the classroom and students would store their work in the appropriate file themselves. Students learned to include the date on their work so that finished work could be compared with earlier drafts. We sent students to the office to photocopy selected pages from recently read books. We stamped a date on the photocopies so that children could be reminded of that momentous transition from picture book to chapter book.

At different times throughout the year, teachers asked children to transfer certain items from their hanging file folders into their individual portfolios. The remaining work was taken home. Students liked the idea that some of their work was being saved in a special place. Soon they began to think of anything special or that marked a step forward as portfolio-worthy. "Can you save this in my portfolio?" asked one first grader pointing with pride to an elaborate construction of blocks. So we began to take Polaroid pictures of block constructions, other large projects, and whole class experiences such as field trips.

We were experimenting. And as teachers do, we each developed different understandings of the content and possibilities of a child's portfolio. The atmosphere was of a learning laboratory, where clinicians were testing hypotheses. We gathered in the faculty lounge or at the photocopier to share what we had learned, then returned to the labs—our classrooms—for further tests. One teacher created "memory photo albums" for each child, lacing together with yarn photos that captured friendships, recess time games, and field trips. Another teacher had the children interview each other about their first days at school, their favorite color and favorite book, their hobbies and career aspirations. The teacher then added a copy of this laminated, spiraled compilation of interviews, along with photos, to each child's portfolio.

Another teacher captured significant events in the life of the classroom on videotape, and again, a copy was included in each child's portfolio.

Together, we tolerated the chaotic nature of this early collecting activity and patiently awaited the yet-to-be-revealed understanding that we hoped would result from the effort. We refrained from making any formal announcements to parents about our exploration of portfolios as we were still very much in the beginning of our thinking. But students realized that we were up to something, and they willingly participated. Children easily identify with the efforts and risks involved in learning something new. They are particularly intuitive in recognizing and supporting learning, especially when it's their teacher's. They enjoy seeing a teacher as like themselves, not completed but evolving.

The Contents of the Portfolio

In the early years of our work we were overly concerned about the specific contents. Although content is a logical way to define a portfolio, we later understood that it's important not to become rigid about what goes into the portfolio. I'm reminded always of the wonderful advice offered by Pearl and Leon Paulsen: "Portfolios tell a story . . . put in anything that helps to tell the story" (1991, p. 294).

As our imaginations fired with ideas of artifacts to be added, the children's portfolios were becoming bulky. The problem was that we didn't know what *not* to include. We had work for every subject area, tapes and photographs, plus the materials garnered by the art teacher—who began to keep separate portfolios for each student that could hold work of various sizes. Programs from Spring Sings were included in many portfolios to remind students of a special role they had played. Evidence of projects and development of skills in Physical Education and Spanish were also part of the portfolio collection.

Nevertheless, we held back from committing ourselves to making a list of what *must* be included. Publications now provide extensive lists of suggested contents for a child's portfolio (Bird, 1992, pp. 122–129; Stevenson, 1992, p. 251), but when we began there was limited literature on the topic. That was fortunate. Although comforting to the beginner, we all know that lists have a way of staying around long after they've outlived their usefulness. It's best to think of the portfolio's contents in a more open-ended way that forces you to keep it alive and fresh and connected to the child.

That can be challenging. Principals and teachers may want to consider engaging in a staff-development activity to consider the contents of the portfolio by placing themselves in the child's role. First imagine that you, like the child, are creating your own portfolio. Your first task is to select an audience. Sample audiences to choose from could be your students, your colleagues, or your administrators. Once you have one audience in mind, jot down three artifacts that you would include in your own portfolio and, most important, your reason for selecting each one. For many years, I've engaged groups of teachers in this exercise. The teachers' responses show how easily teachers can relate to the portfolio decisions confronted by students. "My audience is my students, and I've included some poetry I've written," one teacher offers. "I've chosen my poetry because I'd like my students to know that I'm interested in poetry and that it's part of my life." Another teacher indicates that his audience is his administrator. "I've selected some videotapes of my teaching because I'd like my principal to know that I'm a good teacher." Another teacher who selects her students as audience chooses a vacation photograph of her family canoeing on a lake. "I've selected this picture for my portfolio because I want my students to know who I am outside of school." This warm-up activity can be very helpful in opening up our minds to what can go into the portfolio and why.

Whose Portfolio Is It?

All teachers need to confront the ownership of the portfolio as it arises with each student. "Is this *my* portfolio of teaching supported by you?" or "Is this *your* portfolio of learning supported by me?" is the implicit teacher-to-student question. A portfolio organized to represent a teacher's successful implementation of the grade-level curriculum is an example of teacher ownership. The portfolio that is designed to represent a child's understanding of the story of the year's learning is an example of child ownership. The two will look very different. But in reality, most students' portfolios fall somewhere in between. Both student and teacher contribute to and "own" the portfolio. In addition, it's important to remember that the ratio of teacher to child ownership of the portfolio can vary for each child and teacher as appropriate, and may change as the child matures.

Interrelatedness of Purpose, Ownership, and Content

The purpose, ownership, and content of the portfolio are interrelated issues. Decide any one and the other two will be decided as well. It is the ongoing interplay of our deeper understandings of the answers to each of the following questions that will inform our future uses of portfolios:

- What is the purpose of the portfolio?
- Who owns the portfolio?
- What should go into the portfolio?

The word *portfolio* has a wide range of meanings. Here are just some of the many interpretations I've heard used by teachers or seen in the literature about portfolios. This listing from bottom to top is organized to illustrate stages of ownership of the portfolio.

The most basic definition of a portfolio is a *folder of a child's work*. Most teachers are accustomed to the practice of gathering samples of children's work for the purpose of evaluating progress and assisting the teacher in preparing documents of accountability, for example, report cards. Portfolios understood as a *collection of a child's work* suggest that this student's work is collected over time. It raises issues of judgment about what guides inclusion in the selection.

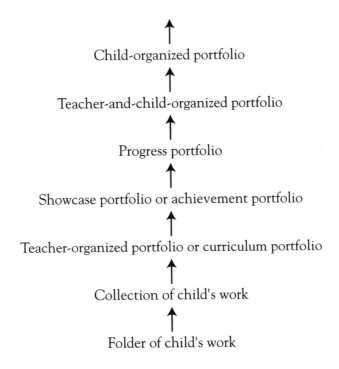

Child-organized portfolio

↑

Teacher-and-child-organized portfolio

↑

Progress portfolio

↑

Showcase portfolio or achievement portfolio

↑

Teacher-organized portfolio or curriculum portfolio

↑

Collection of child's work

↑

Folder of child's work

Stages of Ownership of the Portfolio

A *teacher-organized portfolio* suggests that the teacher is collecting samples of student work organized into categories, most often corresponding to curricular content. A *curriculum portfolio* is much the same as a teacher-organized portfolio, but somewhat different in that content is more clearly defined. The ownership of the portfolio is still under the control of the teacher.

When the teacher organizes a child's work to demonstrate achievement of success in the curriculum, the *achievement portfolio* or *showcase portfolio* brings the issues of content, organization, purpose, and ownership into interplay. The content of the portfolio is customarily defined as the student's best work. Students may be involved in the selection process of the showcase portfolio.

If the contents of the portfolio measures progress rather than simply demonstrating achievement the *progress portfolio* revises some of the issues of content. The teacher remains involved with the organization of the portfolio but contents now include evidence of children's learning in process in place of or in addition to completed and successful work.

As teachers begin to share the ownership of the portfolio with the child by allowing the child to select contents and the reasons for the selection, a new dimension of the portfolio emerges. The *teacher-and-child–organized portfolio* is now commonly used by many teachers. Over time, the recognition that the portfolio belongs to the child significantly alters the role of the teacher in portfolio decisions and introduces alternative ways of thinking about the assessment process.

The *child-organized portfolio* may look very different from the one the teacher would have put together. The child may omit areas of learning where success is not achieved or where interest has not developed. Because the child's view of curriculum is very different from the adult view, the child may choose to include items of significance or achievement related to areas of personal importance. Although a teacher may feel strongly that evidence of successful reading or a perfect math quiz should be part of the portfolio, the child may select a photo of a new friend because making friends is more important to the child than reading or math.

These descriptors are only a small sampling of the many possible labels that identify the concept of portfolio as we move from teacher-organized to child-organized collections. Clearly, these descriptors can be combined to refine the purposes and ownership issues as decided by students and their teachers, for example, a child-organized showcase portfolio. Most students will readily anticipate and adopt an organizational structure that is closely aligned to the organization of school curriculum and teacher expectations. Mindful of their disposition to do so, we need to be watchful for those organizational possibilities not yet fully voiced by a student but evidencing a unique quality that requires our support and encouragement.

These multiple meanings ascribed to *portfolio* have been confusing in the development of this concept. Each of these labels suggests different notions of a portfolio's content, purpose, and creator. In attempting to nail down the definitional boundaries of portfolio we become enmeshed in the triangular framework of purpose, ownership, and content.

These three definitional values for the portfolio are highly interdependent. If one of these values is known the other two will be known as well. When we define the ownership of the portfolio, the purpose and content will be regulated, and so on for each of the three. If the teacher has ownership of the portfolio, its purpose will be to provide evidence of effective teaching of the curriculum and the content will logically consist of teacher-selected artifacts of the child's work in support of that purpose. If the purpose of the portfolio is to supplement lower scores obtained on standardized tests, then it follows that the ownership becomes the teacher's and the content will be selections of successful student work aligned with lower scores on standardized tests.

But if the child is the owner, the purpose will be for the child to relate a personal, unique story of learning and the content will be what the child decides is significant in relating that story. This is a different experience for most teachers. In the early stages of portfolio development, when teachers own the portfolio, we advance in small

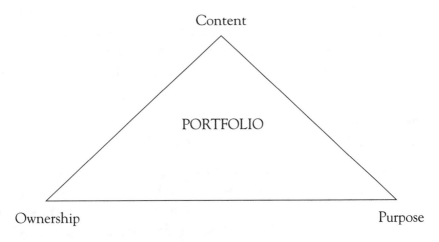

Relationship of Portfolio's Purpose, Ownership, and Content

steps toward predictable ends. Once we involve the child in the process, however, our role shifts from control to facilitation. With children at the helm, supported by teachers, we move into uncharted territory.

Now, however, we have a tool to decipher the way children view their own learning over time. New questions emerge. How does a child comprehend learning? Does a child perceive various learning experiences designed by teachers to relate to one another as, in fact, interconnected? What criteria will a child use (at different ages) for including a sample of work in the portfolio? How do children move from dependence to independence in their ability to structure the portfolio experience? If we can begin to consider that the primary purpose of the portfolio is to provide a vehicle for each child to grow metacognitively and to demonstrate competence in telling the story of learning, the door is open for the child to assume ownership.

There are compromises and trade-offs at every stage of the ownership process. If teachers are in charge of regulating the portfolios, clearly the contents will be more standardized. However, the child may not be able to connect the contents of the portfolio to a personal story of learning. If the child is in charge of the portfolio, the contents are less certain, although our experience has shown that children in charge of their portfolios will often choose evidence of achievement toward stated curriculum goals. The difference is that it is not just the teacher who attributes importance to curriculum goals, but the child. With guidance, children can internalize these goals.

Putting Purpose, Ownership, and Contents in Perspective: What We've Learned

We now know that there is no single, correct portfolio. We have come to understand that the determination of purpose, ownership, and selection of the content of the portfolio is an evolving process shared by child and teacher. At first, children require structure. We advise students about including certain pieces of work that we feel will be valued, if not now, at a later time. We have discovered that the conversations that take place as the early portfolio is being compiled begin to provide a familiar structure. Soon the children feel secure enough to suggest additional entries that are more personal or unique to their own school experience. But even at the earliest stage one message is very clear—we do not assign a letter grade or evaluation to the portfolio. This is not an unusual circumstance in our school district as there are no report cards or letter grades used in our lower schools, but it does indicate the child is the ultimate owner of the portfolio.

Children vary in their ability to assume the role of manager. Some require extensive assistance while others naturally assume a leadership role. Teachers also vary in their ability to let go of the child's portfolio as an indicator of their own teaching skills. As portfolios have become part of our school culture both children and teachers have demonstrated more confidence both in their own ability and in the process of collaborating.

The variables associated with portfolios suggest the richness of their instructional purpose. Children have a natural inclination to collect evidence of their learning. They can internalize meaningful learning goals and see particular samples of their work as evidence of progress toward those goals. But most of all, our students have shown us that they are genuinely excited about taking responsibility for collecting their own work.

Reflection Tag

I chose this piece for my portfolio because . . .

It explains how to use reflection tags. The student considers reasons for including a piece of work in the portfolio and records why it matters or how it relates to other pieces of work. Developing children's strategies for thinking about their work is the most powerful rationale for portfolios.

LESSON 5

Portfolios Encourage Children to Think About Their Learning

The gathering of student work engendered many thoughtful exchanges and conversations between students and their teachers. As selections were considered for the portfolio, children made comments that expressed awareness of their own strategies for learning. They distinguished between work that was easy for them and work that was a challenge. We realized that these insights were an important aspect of each child's story of learning. Finding a way for children to connect their own metacognitive insights to samples of their work was another big challenge. Our next step was to move from collection to reflection.

Metacognition, knowing what we know and how we have come to know it, is now understood to be an essential component of education. Researchers recognize children's awareness of their own cognitive processes as an important factor in how youngsters use learning strategies, and one that will affect future task performance and outcomes (Bereiter and Scardamalia, 1983; Fry and Lupart, 1987; Hinchcliffe and Roberts, 1987; McCombs, 1987; Wolf and Reardon, 1996). To control these metacognitive processes, children need to be introduced to the language of self-reflection. In addition to language, young students need to develop a repertoire of cognitive experiences where the connection between the process and the task has been directly specified for them.

Portfolios: A Curriculum for Thinking About Learning

Portfolios can be a central curricular framework for the development of a child's metacognitive awareness (Gordon and Bonilla-Brown, 1996, p. 39). When young children are given the opportunity to review, compare, and attribute value to selections of their own work they are immersed in metacognitive decisions. As they think about the conditions that were present when particular work was completed, they realize how best to replicate that same quality of work in the future.

> I think I'm a good reader when I don't read too fast. I read as fast as I can so [long as] I don't mix up words. Sometimes when I'm reading to myself I go so fast that I don't really understand. When I come upon something that doesn't make sense, I reread the passage very slowly.
>
> —*Paul, fifth grade*

How do you know how you're learning? This is a question that should be considered in the education of young children—a question for the child as well. As children grow taller and heavier, they have direct evidence of these changes through measurement. Students can take tests and compare present and prior scores to have some idea of what they've learned. But by what means do you know how you learn? This question examines the conditions and requirements for learning and the learner's awareness of those conditions and requirements. It requires knowing which strategies you use to obtain and retain information and how to make them available for future problem solving. Portfolios can illuminate these cognitive pathways so that children gain deeper insight about themselves as learners.

As children consider the connections between particular pieces of work and what they did to produce them, conversations with their teacher serve to solidify those metacognitive associations. The resultant confidence gained from *knowing how they know* has direct relevance to ongoing learning experiences.

Reflective Conversation Promotes Metacognition: The Theory

The link between metacognition and portfolio is reflective conversation. Progress reports that include children's own thinking about their work as expressed in portfolios that have been influenced by reflective conversations with teachers, provide a means for both the child and the teacher to understand the learning process. When child and teacher discuss specific learning experiences the child senses the importance of thinking about these things for oneself.

TEACHER: Which of these books was most difficult for you?

ASHLEY (IN FIRST GRADE): This book . . . because it has lots of words that I don't know.

TEACHER: What do you do when you come across a word you don't know?

ASHLEY: If there are no pictures, then it's hard. . . .

TEACHER: Can you think of a way to figure out the word?

ASHLEY: Sometimes you find the next word kind of hooks on to the word you don't know . . . then you know what that word means . . . it goes with that word when you read ahead . . . if you can go on to the next word and look at that and sometimes it hooks on to the words that are difficult . . . but if it's not like that then it's hard.

TEACHER: That's important that you know that . . . good readers do just what you said.

Ted Sizer, in his book *Horace's School*, emphasized the importance of thoughtful conversation in establishing an environment in which students are collaborative partners with their teachers (1992, Chapter 7). Sizer suggests that the quality of that conversation sets a standard by which the ongoing adult-and-child interactions can be measured. Fred Newmann, of the University of Wisconsin, includes "substantive conversation" as a key component of assessment (1991, p. 461). For Newmann, a substantive conversation occurs when a child has an opportunity to express a view, an insight, or a connection between prior and present learning, and an adult responds to that view in a reflective manner.

Carl Bereiter and Marlene Scardamalia focus on the importance of conversation in the development of children's metacognitive understandings. They view the child as "co-investigator" with the teacher as the two strive, through conversation, to construct useful strategies for learning (1983, p. 62). Conversation is a primary tool for teaching specific strategies of self-evaluation to children. In describing the kind of adult-child interaction that encourages children to talk about their thoughts about learning, Bereiter and Scardamalia provide specific guidelines for adult interviewers to develop techniques that elicit this kind of conversation with children. They remind us that "when a child is telling us something that seems insignificant or very confused, we are probably missing something very important . . . the child is probably struggling to explain something at the edge of current awareness (p. 67). Assisting children in mapping out their cognitive development has far-reaching consequences for the students as they develop intellectual maturity.

> Such coinvestigation . . . holds promise . . . at the level of direction and purpose. Students cannot be expected to take a self-directive role in their cognitive development unless they themselves, and not just the teachers, have a sense of where development is heading—where the growing edge of their competence is and what possibilities lie ahead. Studying theories of developmental psychology is not likely to give students such knowledge in a usable form. Active investigation of their own cognitive strategies could do so, however— especially if it is done in collaboration with an adult who can help recognize and reflect upon what is happening and help them experiment with possible next stages in development [Bereiter and Scardamalia, 1983, pp. 79–80].

Sophie Haroutunian-Gordon devoted an entire book to the subject of teaching through conversation in the high school setting. She found that personal events in the lives of urban high school students resonated with and allowed for "powerful encounters with universal themes of literature" and that discussing those connections helped the students make sense of their life experiences as well as of the curriculum (1991, p. 7).

In all these portrayals of successful learning environments, it is considered essential to give children means by which they can express and expand their understanding of their own learning processes. We need to provide children with specific tools of metacognition if they are to be a part of this process. The portfolio is a particularly powerful tool to accomplish this goal. Portfolios provide an important opportunity for students to express their individual voice and to give evidence of their metacognitive understanding about learning. To accomplish those tasks, concentrated interactive conversation is needed at both the selection and reflection stages of the portfolio-building process. Reflective conversation takes on added significance when connected to the ongoing activity required to create a useful portfolio.

In addition to the benefits afforded through conversation, the motivational opportunities provided by portfolios are also an important factor. In exploring motivational aspects of learning to read and write, Cheryl Spaulding discusses the role of intrinsic motivation, which she views as the by-product of the self-perception of competence and self-determination. Spaulding explains that "when individuals perceive themselves as being capable of completing a specific task or engaging in a specific endeavor and they perceive themselves as having some degree of control over that task or endeavor, then they are likely to be intrinsically motivated to engage in that task or endeavor. Conversely, if either of these perceptions is not present, intrinsic motivation is also likely to be missing" (1991, p. 180).

If we borrow this understanding of intrinsic motivation and apply it to children's assessment of their own learning, we would direct our instructional energies to provide children with an authentic sense of ownership and control in their assessment of their work as well as teaching specific strategies of evaluation to children to achieve competence in assessing their own learning over time.

Creating and repeatedly interacting with portfolios provides children with chances to reflect on their work, see what they're doing when they succeed, and recognize what they're interested in and good at. Presentation of a portfolio to a selected audience such as parents engages the child in a substantive conversation that further supports insights and self-knowledge required for the presentation of self to the world.

Moving from Theory to Practice: Introducing Portfolios to Children

Children love being in charge. They readily identify tasks and projects that are of interest to them and that involve some mark of status. Being the line leader or taking the attendance to the office or collecting last night's homework are among the long list of responsibilities that children readily gravitate to, and that reinforce pleasure in doing meaningful work and belonging to a community.

Children find it natural to be in charge of collecting evidence of their learning. It satisfies a human need for responsibility, and for engaging in necessary and purposeful work. For the younger students, it helps to connect the idea of portfolio with the notion of a baby book—as long as the teacher adds, "But you're not babies anymore, so we'll call this collection a *portfolio.*" Children like the sound of this grown-up word and are intrigued by its meaning—as yet not fully understood.

Much like their teachers, the children need to engage in the physicality and concreteness of the portfolio before they can begin to appreciate the abstract qualities of its purpose. It begins with language—a word—*portfolio.* And then a visual. For the first grader, a 9.5"x14.5" red folder. "This will be the folder for your first grade portfolio. What goes in this folder? You will decide and I will help you."

At this point, the instructional conversation can progress in many different directions. The teacher should feel guided by instinct, by the metacognitive readiness of this particular group of students, and by any specific purpose determined by the teacher or group of teachers. There is no single, correct way to present portfolios to children, but because the concept is so natural teachers will discover a wide variety of strategies and activities that will successfully introduce the idea. The following examples of portfolio introduction activities are coordinated with the discussion of ownership of the portfolio as the teacher moves from exclusive manager of the portfolio to facilitator. How you present the idea of portfolios to your students is directly connected to your current notion of ownership. We have found that the understanding of ownership changes over time.

To get started, choose an activity that is manageable for you and a particular group of students. All these activities can be adjusted for students of different ages.

- Show the students a sample portfolio that includes the format and content that you would like your students to replicate.

- Select one subject area such as math and direct the students to select a sample of their best work. The portfolio is of course much more than a collection of best work, but it may be something the child will be proud to include. Follow this same format for other subject areas to be included in the portfolio.

- Select one subject area such as writing and direct the students to collect a sample from the beginning of the school year and a current sample of writing. For reading, have the students put a Post-it note on a page from a book they were reading in the beginning of the year and do the same for a book they are currently reading. Pages from these books can be photocopied and date stamped to highlight changes in reading skill development.

- Select one subject area such as writing and engage the students in a conversation about "How should we select pieces of writing for our portfolios?" The group conversation will allow students to hear different perspectives from their peers that may stimulate further ideas. In addition, the teacher will be able to assess the metacognitive maturity of the group, and in response can engage in specific conversations that will assist individual students in elaborating on their own thinking.

- Invite older students to present their portfolios to your students. Young children are delighted to hear from these older boys and girls—because they're genuinely interested in what they have to say, and also because it helps the younger children feel safer in interacting with the older students in less secure settings like on the playground or on the bus. Older students may also be helpful in assisting the teacher by participating in individual conversations. An older child with a specific interest in science may help younger students with a similar interest. Students who once struggled to organize materials will be flattered when they are asked to help younger children who are having difficulty with the basics of the selecting activity.

- Invite the art teacher or parents with portfolios of their own to talk to your class about them. Hearing how an architect or a financial manager or a carpenter thinks about a portfolio is very helpful to children of all ages. It heightens the child's awareness to the variety of materials portfolios can contain as well as the process that different people engage in as they select the contents of their portfolio.

Once you and the students have decided on the structure of their portfolios, you will want to introduce the idea of reflection upon prior and present learning. "What do you notice?" is a good theme question when children are examining their work. Transferring their skills of observation from one subject to another allows them to act like detectives and discover their skills and strategies for learning. As noted, a very useful activity for stimulating this conversation is to photocopy a page of text that a student was reading at the beginning of the year and a page of text from a current book, and ask, "What do you notice?" or "What differences do you observe?" Children readily note the clues that provide evidence of their growing reading skills. "There are more words on the page"—"The print is smaller"—"This book is wider"—"I was afraid to try this book at first"—"There aren't as many pictures in this book"—"The pictures help me know the words"—"I still need help with the longer sentences"—"I use my bookmark to cover up the rest of the page"—these are some of the metacognitive observations that encourage children to witness and make sense of their learning.

Attaching Words to Thoughts

Of primary importance is the child's experience of putting words to their observations. Language is necessary to the development of meta-cognitive awareness.

> Sometimes when I am reading information books I come across something that doesn't make sense to me or a word that I don't know the meaning of. When that happens I either look it up in the dictionary or ask my teacher. It usually only happens when I'm reading information books.
>
> —*Laura, fifth grade*

Classmates can be good detectives for each other as well. One second grade teacher asked her students to exchange writing folders so that classmates could record their observations of others' writings over the course of the year. Children enjoy receiving notes from a classmate and they also enjoy "being the teacher" and so they eagerly engage in this reflective activity:

To William:
I notices that your storys are getting longer. I have also noticed that you have been drawing with one coler. Your handwriting is getting better.

—*From Ray, second grade*

To Diane:
I think you ar getting much better at writing then before the year. I like the storie about your cat. You relly emproved in

your handwriting. And before you did capatal letters on the
end of the sentens.

—*From Jerry, second grade*

This classroom exercise allowed students to experience peer
observations of the writing process that are particular to this age of
student. Children talking to children about their learning is an enormously powerful adjunct to children's self-awareness. Of invaluable
importance is the chance for the teacher to get inside the seven-
year-old mind and discern what they notice about the writing process. Knowing the benchmarks of improvement as perceived by the
child is a vital tool for effective teaching.

Reflection Tags Inject Thoughtfulness into the Portfolio

As we gained more experience with students collecting their work,
we began to realize the broad scope of this project. Some students
saved everything. Others were overwhelmed by the decisions involved. We needed a mechanism to assist students and ourselves in
managing the size of their portfolios and, more important, to inject
more thoughtfulness into the selection process. The idea of *reflection
tags* quickly worked its way around the building. The basic idea is to
write down a reason for including a piece of work on an individual
tag and attach it to the corresponding sample of student work. This
idea is usually presented in a rugtime discussion with students. A
teacher might say something along these lines:

> Let's think of some of the reasons you might choose a piece
> of your work to include in your portfolio. When you think of
> a reason, raise your hand and I'll list them on the board.
> [Pause to collect some reasons and write them out.] I have
> some blank tags for you on the table; at the top each tag says
> "I chose this piece for my portfolio because:" and there's a
> blank line for you to fill in. Take a look at the board for some

reasons you may choose a piece. You may think of other ideas once you get started. That's fine—these ideas on the board are not the only reasons for choosing. When you find a piece of work you want to save, complete a reflection tag and staple it to that piece like this. [Demonstrating stapling to upper left corner of work.]

The physical act of attaching a reflection tag to a piece of work stimulates the metacognitive connection of how that particular entry fits into the child's chronology of learning. The opportunity to review these reflection tags over a period of years helps young students to identify curricular interests and realize their achievements. In examining one child's reflections on samples of his writing over a five-year period, we can begin to see the evolution of his interest in writing.

I chose this piece for my portfolio because . . .
As a first grader: "I lik to writ"
As a second grader: "I like writing. . . . You can write down your thoughts or what you are imagining."
As a third grader: "I like to write real stories about my life. Now I can write what I mean."
As a fourth grader: "My writing is improving . . . because I'm working hard at it. I've been making more complex sentences and using more detail. I've learned where you put punctuation and what it means."
As a fifth grader: "I've become better at revising my stories. My greatest strength is being able to put my thoughts together nicely. . . . I think I know what to put where."
—*Charlie, first through fifth grade*

These reflection tags can serve as a metacognitive history. That is, a child could examine the tags over time and discern metacognitive trends that would assist in making significant decisions about future learning or career choices.

Reflection Tag

I chose this piece for my portfolio because . . .

Portfolios are useful for all students—whatever their capacities
in the various subjects of the curriculum. The elasticity of
portfolios helps us identify and support individual learning
needs and interests. Over and over again, children show us
that portfolios are natural for them.

LESSON 6

Portfolios Respond to the Individual Needs of Students

Children learn in different ways and at different rates. They are most likely to attain skills and achieve competence at unannounced times through projects and assignments that matter to them. The portfolio is a tool that can capture a child's imagination and accommodate a wide range of children's abilities and interests. The portfolio organizes, instructs, reinforces, and suggests connections between prior, present, and future learning.

The inclusion of *all* children in the learning and assessment process is fundamental to the consideration of children as competent. Portfolios are exceptionally useful in supporting children with special education needs as well as in challenging students who absorb information quickly and need supplements to the grade-level curriculum. Portfolios allow all children to be successful in organizing the story of their own learning.

Portfolios Can Facilitate Inclusion

Emily is seated at her desk between her parents. Her arms are crossed on her chest in a pose identical to her father's. They are smiling at each other lovingly. It is Portfolio Evening and all the third grade students are anxious to show their schoolwork to their parents. They have been preparing their presentations for weeks. Emily, who has been enrolled in our school for one year, is a student with Down's syndrome. As she opens her portfolio Emily begins to signal to her parents through pointing, smiling, and a few words, that certain items in this collection of her schoolwork have meaning to her. She gazes across the classroom and sees her classmates in similar interaction with their own parents. Although the contents of Emily's portfolio are quite different from those of her peers, the process she is going through is identical. She is beginning to develop a critical sense of her learning and to communicate her observations to her parents.

As I observe this third grade Portfolio Conference Evening, I recall that Emily had been excluded from the mandated state testing administered a few weeks before. Her participation in that testing would have been meaningless, as it would not have furthered either our understanding of Emily as a learner or Emily's own sense of herself as a student. What was equally evident to me on that Portfolio Evening was how naturally she participated in the review of her own portfolio for her parents and how mutually meaningful this form of assessment was, as her parents, teacher, principal, and peers could observe Emily's critical consideration of her own schoolwork. At some level, Emily understood that, too, as her smile conveyed to me when I entered the classroom.

What is important to understand about this vignette is that Portfolio Conference Evenings were a part of our school culture before Emily came to us. The structure of the experience itself, that is, the Portfolio Evening, had been clearly designed to be an experience equally as beneficial to Emily as to her peers. Many special needs children are offered the "accommodation of exclusion" from standardized testing as an acknowledgment of the tests' inability to capture multiple ways of learning. Through the experience of portfolios, on the other hand, all children are allowed to gain insights into their own learning, each one at the level of individual capability.

The flexibility and versatility of the concept of portfolios makes it a useful tool for engaging students of all abilities as they examine the process and products of their learning. A portfolio can be organized in tandem with a student's Individualized Education Plan (IEP) and focused on basic components that provide necessary repetition and rehearsal of skills for the special needs student. Alternatively, the portfolio can be expanded and elaborated to challenge students who benefit from extending the classroom curriculum into specialized advanced projects.

Portfolios Support Independent Learning Projects

Stephen is only seven years old and he is a playwright. He has an extensive résumé already. He has assembled repertory groups in the Let's Pretend Room of his Kindergarten class and the Block Corner of first grade. But during Snack Time Theater in his second grade classroom, his talents have flourished. Stephen is now taking on a production of "The Wiz." With music in his head and an eye for costume coordination, Stephen examines the wardrobe possibilities in the Dress-Up Corner. His classmates are giddy in anticipation of the roles Stephen will choose for them. Memorizing a script is especially important in this small repertory group as some of the players have not yet learned how to read. Everyone has a role in the production whether as actor, stage crew, or audience. With only a few recess-time rehearsals, the final production has two performances scheduled in the auditorium. And all this flurry of dramatic activity takes place in only a few days. That is how the briefly sustained interest of the seven-year-old operates. Among the other second graders this spontaneous production is a hit.

On the Portfolio Evening following the premiere of his production, Stephen proudly reviews some artifacts of the play along with his parents. The printed program, photos, costume design sketches, and drafts of his script are all contained in his portfolio. These souvenirs are props for the animated conversation that Stephen is having with his parents about that memorable event and about other, future production ideas that are just occurring to him. It is that connection between prior, present, and future learning that is best portrayed within the portfolio and that affirms the immeasurable value of this experience for each child. The importance of the specific contents of the portfolio is best assessed by the narrator of the story—the child. Each entry serves as a representative event in that child's story of learning. In that way, the portfolio functions as a record of the development of the metacognitive voice of the child.

Portfolios Are a Repository for Prior Topics of Interest

Ben needs a topic for his research report. A list of suggested topics from his teacher has no appeal for him. Nor is he the only fifth grader in his class who has come to the unhappy conclusion that at ten years of age he has absolutely no interest worthy of pursuing in a research report. Ben's teacher, not totally surprised by this fifth grade dilemma, sends this small band of reluctant researchers off to the Archive in the Library/Resource Center to retrieve their own archives—of previous years' portfolios—that may include evidence of a prior interest. Returning to their classroom with their portfolios of the past five years, this small group of students begins to review the contents of their collections.

Ben dwells on the contents of his first grade portfolio. He reexamines some well-executed sketches of jet fighter planes and he remembers working very hard on these pictures after finding a great book about aircraft in the library. His classmate Norman, seated nearby, notices Ben's find and offers a reminiscent "oh yeah" as he remembers when he and Ben were in that same first grade classroom. Ben presented these drawings when he was Person of the Week. Both boys giggle as they remember being first graders. They continue to talk about jet fighter planes for a while, comparing sizes of engines and speeds of flight. "You should do your report on these jets," Norman suggests, and returns to his own archive in hopes of finding a research report topic for himself.

The notion of revisiting the portfolio archive for prior topics of interest is natural for children. Simple sketches, stories, and photographs of past events and projects stimulate renewed interest at a deeper and more mature level. The archive is filled with stories that can be developed, pictures that capture important moments, and ideas that can be extended.

Portfolios Promote Tolerance for Learning Differences

A serendipitous benefit of portfolios as well as the celebration of portfolio conferences is the simultaneous focus on the individual child and the reflective experience of all the children in the class-room. Most children's awareness of how they're doing is derived ex-clusively through standardized tests. This is, for the most part, an exercise that separates children into distinct ability groups. Chil-dren experience standardized tests as a means to sort the competent and the less competent. Such testing encourages them to view their own learning and that of their peers as fitting into a high, medium, or low level of performance according to preordained expectations of these measures. In addition, with increased media attention fo-cused on publishing school scores in local newspapers, children come to view their schools as fitting into these same hierarchical categories.

Portfolios, on the other hand, counterbalance that external stan-dard with an internal standard of expectation excellence. Differences in learning products or processes are obvious—but in the context of portfolios, these disparities are not thought of as a mechanism to des-ignate a particular category of competence. By attributing value to the unique ways in which children demonstrate their learning, teach-ers encourage children to strive for their personal best and to be ac-countable for a deeper understanding of how that goal was achieved. In that way, portfolios model and sustain a more inclusive and hu-mane disposition toward learning.

Competitive sorting according to ability is a reality in our educa-tional lives. So is reflection on the connections of prior, present, and future learning. But the latter is vastly underrepresented in our ways of conceiving of grading or evaluating students. The "accommodation of exclusion" that is provided for handicapped students is a peculiar concept that deserves further attention from educators and policy-makers as we develop more appropriate ways of assessing children's learning. In that same vein, the attainment of a perfect score on a standardized test provides us with only a very gross portrayal of skills and content already achieved. It offers no direction as to the interests and projects that might sustain the motivation of a high-achieving student.

The values associated with portfolios move us beyond sending children to different classrooms to be assessed, or grouping children according to subject area competence. The shift from an external standard of achievement to an internal monitoring of self-assessment is a skill that all students will need to develop as they mature and engage in their life's work. With portfolios, we have an opportunity to incorporate this larger life goal into our assessment practices.

The Portfolio Experience Across the Grade Levels

We have noted that particular skills of organization and reflection appear to develop naturally at certain ages. The achievement of these developmental milestones across the grade levels readies the children for new metacognitive tasks and a deeper understanding of what their portfolio can be. Beginning in Kindergarten the students are introduced to different dimensions of the portfolio experience.

Kindergarten

In Kindergarten children are reminded of the baby books that their parents have put together, so as to introduce the concepts of purposeful selection, life history, and evidence of personal change over time. Paintings, drawings, writing, and many photos of each Kindergartner are collected by the teacher throughout the year and placed in manila folders. Toward the end of the year conversations with the teacher begin the process of revisiting, reviewing, and selection. Children select photos of important memories or particular pieces of work. They tell their teacher their reasons why a picture is important to them. These conversations serve to illuminate the important events of the Kindergarten year as noted by the child.

The accomplishment of building a block structure and making new friendships is a valued benchmark for the five-year-old child.

I am making a castle with my friends
                        —*Amy, Kindergarten*

First Grade

The first grader may already have a lot of information about portfolios from older brothers and sisters. The first grade teachers again remind their young students of their baby books. "Now that you're in first grade *you* will select some of your first grade work and we'll keep it in a portfolio." The first graders love the sound of this grown-up word and remember that their Kindergarten teachers introduced this idea to them last year.

The task of the first grader is to learn how to reflect. This important goal is embedded in the curriculum. Teacher questions that encourage this metacognitive thinking cause the children to consider what kinds of learning tasks are hard for them, what tasks they understand easily, and what skills they need to accomplish some tasks.

"What's hardest for you in reading?"

"How do you know you have improved in writing?"

"In science, what does it mean to be a good observer?"

"What do you think you're good at?"

These kinds of inquiries move the child beyond predictable selections of "best work" or a piece of work that was completely correct. Beginning appreciation of the process of learning is introduced in first grade. To capture the richness of children's thinking as they explain their reasons for their selections, first grade teachers take down the exact words on reflection tags that are attached to the corresponding piece of work.

Oftentimes fourth or fifth grade student "learning buddies" assist the children in sorting out their work and selecting items for their portfolio. These older students also act as scribes for their young friends and record the wording for their reflection tags.

I know my writing has improved this year because . . . "At the beginning of the year I only wrote about 2 or 3 words and the letters were not right. Now I can space words and I can put periods at the end and I can put capitals."

—*Billy, first grade*

The best part of first grade is . . . "you get to go to lots of places."

—*Lily, first grade*

The most important thing I learned in math this year was . . . "time . . . it's important so you know what time to go to bed or to see a movie."

—*Devin, first grade*

The story I am reading is . . . "The School" I like this story because . . . "it seems real." I picked this page because . . . "I like making friends and making friends is important to me."

—*Lauren, first grade*

Second Grade

In second grade, children may be asked, "Why would you put something in your portfolio?" "Because it's my best work" is usually the first response. With patience, the teacher elicits further value statements from the students. "Because I'm proud of it," or "Because I didn't think I could do this," or "Because I worked very hard on it." The teacher records these thoughts and values on tags of paper and asks the children to affix them to particular entries in their portfolio. "Do you have any blank tags?" asks another student, demonstrating that further ideas have occurred about why one keeps artifacts in a portfolio, and indicating that the transfer of ownership from teacher to child has begun. Open-ended written reflection about the content is an important element in the construction of a portfolio. The physical act of attaching meaning to a specific piece of work contributes significantly to the child's metacognitive growth.

In second grade, children learn to organize their work into folders and to write their own reflections. As children's spoken language is far more sophisticated than their written language, many of the reflection tags will show the major challenge of recording their own thoughts in writing. Many students at this age are comfortable with the phrase of "I chose this piece for my portfolio because I liked it." However, in conversation, the spoken language of their insights is far more developed.

I chose this piece for my portfolio because . . . "it has real seeds on it . . . we had to dig in the fruit to get them."
—*Anna, second grade*

I chose this piece for my portfolio because . . . "it was the last page of my writing journal and it shows how much I improved."
—*Sam, second grade*

I chose this piece for my portfolio because . . . "it was my own idea."
—*David, second grade*

Third Grade

Third grade students begin to consider alternative options for organizing their portfolio—by date, by subject, by interest, or by favorites. The written language of their reflection tags is coming to approximate their spoken language. Goal setting is an important part of the third grade portfolio experience. As children reflect on their past years of work teachers guide them in assessing goals for the current year and linking portfolios to personal goals.

I chose this piece for my portfolio because . . . "it's about sports. My strength is sports and spelling. I think that's because I love doing them both."
—*Charlie, third grade*

I chose this piece for my portfolio because . . . "it's a biography of Dr. Martin Luther King Jr. and I worked really hard on it. . . . my mom was proud of me."

—Sara, third grade

I chose this piece for my portfolio because . . . "I don't count on my fingers anymore like I did last year."

—Katie, third grade

Fourth Grade

Fourth graders work to refine the language of self-reflection. Their portfolio work is focused on the awareness of personal qualities and abilities that promote learning. In addition they write reflective responses to questions about their skills as a learner. By fourth grade the concept of portfolio as "telling the story of my learning" is embedded in the curriculum.

I chose this piece for my portfolio because . . . "I love writing! My vocabulary has improved pretty much. The stories I have written come to life. They seem to pop right out of my head and into my notebook. I understand my stories better. This story fits together. Also I find the more I write the more my imagination stretches."

—Maddie, fourth grade

Fifth Grade

By fifth grade, students are able to analyze, assess, and note growth patterns in their portfolios. In designing a table of contents or a longer narrative description of the contents of the portfolio, students examine the accumulated artifacts, assign value, and begin to assess the trend line of their learning. They compare pages of text with large print and illustrations mastered in first grade and compare it to the historical novel they are currently reading. They pluck out writing pieces with large penciled letters and invented spelling from their first grade year, and smile as they consider their current level of mastery as evidenced in the final draft of their research report. Finer distinctions of growth are made as these students examine and compare work from the beginning of the current school year with present projects. In fifth grade, students are able to produce more lengthy reflective essays that evidence their more mature and still very joyful thoughts about learning.

> I think school is great. Not only is it fun but you're learning. Science is my favorite subject. I like real hands-on science. Last year in Social Studies I did a report on Georgia. It was the largest project I had ever done in my life. This year I did a report on steam trains. The quality of my work is better this year. It went smoother. My spelling has improved. I spell words the way they sound. For example I will spell "group" like "grupe" because that makes sense. Sometimes it's right and sometimes it's wrong. Math is not my favorite subject. I think that I need to slow down because I'm going too fast and getting the answers wrong. If I did slow down I could probably get things right the first time.
>
> —C. J., *fifth grade*

Summing Up

At each grade level, we have found that portfolios provide rich opportunities for teachers and students to engage in reflective conversations that stimulate metacognitive development. The insights that children glean from focused and structured review of their work are invaluable to them in understanding their own interests and dispositions for learning. The excitement that children demonstrate about organizing their work and taking ownership of their learning is evident. This led naturally to one more step. We soon realized that to secure and solidify the benefits of these metacognitive exchanges, we needed an audience and an event. In addition, we needed a place to keep these ever-growing collections of children's school history.

Reflection Tag

I chose this piece for my portfolio because . . .

How a school or classroom looks and feels to a child is connected to feelings of self-reliance required for a meaningful portfolio experience. The organization of classroom space can enhance the sense of ownership and control of the environment—an important element in a child's learning.

LESSON 7

Designating a Space and Place for Gathering Memories

Recently a former student, now a college freshman, stopped by school to visit his second grade sister's classroom. As we chatted briefly in the hallway about how the school looked smaller to him now, I asked him if he knew which classroom was Connie's. He smiled and pointed down the main hallway. "The room with the yellow door: How could I forget?"

That smile reminded me that he, too, had been in that very same classroom as a second grader. It also reminded me how important it is for a young child to be saved from peer embarrassment by being confidently able to remember which classroom door to go to each morning. Such a simple idea—painting the doors red, yellow, or blue so that children feel secure in knowing their own classrooms. This example illustrates what a school building itself *can* communicate. Space and how it is organized has a profound effect upon both learning and the humanly felt sense of being connected to a place. A good space anticipates a child's needs and signals respect for that child as an individual.

The Message of Environment

In recent years the school environment has been recognized as an important component contributing to children's behavior and the success of a child's learning. The look and feel of school is deeply connected to attitudes and behavior. A child's self-esteem, sense of belonging, and conflicting needs for control over the world and for boundaries to guide that control can be shaped through the thoughtful design of the school and classroom. When children experience a school obviously designed with their needs in mind, they notice it and they make use of it. We have observed children over the years demonstrate a more natural disposition to engage in reflective conversations about their learning. We attribute this disposition, in part, to the secure feeling created by the design of space in our school.

There are specific features of the Crow Island design that promote respectful behavior, enhance learning, and honor children. The lowered classroom ceilings create an intimate classroom space suitable for small children. Two windowed walls in every classroom invite the outdoors inside. Each classroom includes an outside door to a separate courtyard space for children to observe their plantings or simply experience a restful moment. All classrooms have an L-shaped floor plan that includes an adjacent workroom area to facilitate large block designs, science centers, ongoing projects, or to serve as a technology center in the intermediate-level classrooms. And as noted, every hallway door is vividly announced in one of the three primary colors to highlight each classroom's relative location. Wide hallways accommodate a feeling of personal space as children move about the building throughout the day. Skylights bring additional natural light into these hallways, which can also be used as adjacent student work areas when needed. Even when first graders are painting large murals in the hall there is still sufficient space for another class to pass without interfering with the work. Classroom walls of ponderosa pine have been stapled into for years as teachers display children's work.

The celebration of Crow Island's fiftieth anniversary in the fall of 1990 provided a unique opportunity to collect adults' reflections of their experiences when they were students. Over four hundred alumni responded to a questionnaire that asked them to offer significant memories of their time at Crow Island, and specifically, the effect of the design of the building on their early learning. The recollections of these alums were rich with memories of the building and its impact. Again and again, these former students recalled vignettes that highlight the importance of the physical space and its connection to their early school memories.

The thoughtfulness of a scaled design was deeply felt by these young students. Students recall, for example, that "the light switches were at my level and the auditorium had benches starting with the little ones in front . . . everything was within my reach." "The seats in the auditorium fit me. My feet could touch the floor and this is important when you feel small." The open feel of having two walls of windows and the convenience of having a bathroom in *every* classroom is not lost on young children. One alum tells us that "the huge windows and the wooded view stimulated imagination and creativity . . . I first learned to ask 'how' and 'why' at Crow Island School and I'm still doing so." Another former student recalls, "I liked *not* having to raise my hand and walk down a hallway when I had to go to the bathroom." Three separate age-level playgrounds allow children to feel safe in their play area and confident that they can risk acquiring new skills without the intrusion of a much older and possibly less sympathetic student. Former students remember that on the playground "kids were my size and I felt safe."

These alumni recollections tell us that the intent to communicate certain values was successfully accomplished by the architects and educators who collaborated in the design of our school. A building that communicates respect to those who use it was an important goal of the designers. The *autonomy* of the young child is reinforced through scaled front steps, scaled auditorium benches, light switches and door handles on a child's level. Stimulation of the child's *imagination* was considered when the actual site of the building, adjacent to a wooded area, was selected. *Experimentation* is invited in the designation of a workroom space in every classroom.

Issues of space, accessibility, innovative design, and thoughtful planning for children are directly connected to the portfolio experience. Thoughtfully designed spaces for learning have the power to evoke the dispositions required to engage in reflective assessment of learning. Schools do not need to be rebuilt to accomplish this goal. Within any individual classroom, materials and furniture can be arranged in ways that communicate independence, accessibility, and a spirit of experimentation.

Creating private nooks or enclosed areas surrounded by a bookcase and a room divider gives children a feeling of control over the space. Colorful pillows, a small table, and a lamp add warmth and make an inviting space for a child to compose some reflections. Wide-open rug areas or hallways provide the necessary space to lay out samples of work. Shelving units or drawers or hanging file folders that are accessible to the children as designated places for their own papers and folders is another way of supporting the emergent autonomy and responsibility in each child.

The Creation of an Archive

The school was clearly a special place: Now we wanted to make the children feel special themselves within the context of the school. Finding a place for gathering memories and treasured samples of schoolwork can be challenging. After a year or two of collecting children's work, we had to search for a place to keep the large collections that were being maintained in each classroom. Our faculty discussions emphasized the importance of children's having access to their work over time, so that they could develop a better understanding of their history as a student. We had decided to use the term *portfolio* when referring to a single year's selection of works and *archive* for the total collection, which could span up to six years in our K–5 school. But where could we store such an unwieldy bundle of student history? Securing a place for children's memories came about in this way.

Two teachers and I were in a taxi headed for Washington National Airport, proud to see the monuments of our country's history. Every landmark reminded us of the separate personal efforts that are woven together to comprise a single national story. Although weary from an all-day meeting and looking forward to our trip home, we were energized by a palpable sense of our connection to this much larger story of our heritage.

We had come to Washington with questions, but after attending a conference on authentic assessment, we were returning to Chicago with those questions unanswered. It was clear to us in that ballroom full of educators that our understanding about what student portfolios could be was quite different from the notions of other teachers. This was a hot topic in education at that time and we were hoping to find an intellectual structure for our own beginning understanding of portfolios. Our discomfort increased, however, as the presenters talked more about what standardized tests don't do than what portfolios could do.

With a burst of private boastfulness in the backseat of that taxicab, we acknowledged that our preliminary work with portfolios at Crow Island School was going in a positive direction. Our faculty and students had already committed a few years of discussion and lab work to portfolios. We were seeking refinements of our project to bring along our ever-deepening understanding. And as we captured our final glimpses of Washington's monuments and memorials, we decided that we needed a place for all of the portfolios—a central location that would elevate the significance of the portfolio archive.

Gathering all our vignettes and artifacts of learning in one location would attribute importance to this schoolwide project. On a more practical note, this idea could address the growing concern of many teachers who found classroom storage unwieldy. But where in the school could we establish an archive? The faculty lounge was quickly dismissed because students don't go to the faculty lounge and therefore the location of the portfolio archive would send a message inconsistent with our idea of the portfolio belonging to the child. The backstage area of the auditorium was eliminated because it was not a part of the building that resonated with our intentions. One of us finally suggested our Library/Resource Center and this idea was immediately supported by the other two. We couldn't quite imagine where the shelving for literally hundreds of large red-roped envelopes would go but we knew this would be the right place. We were confident that our Resource Center director would find a way—though none of us was anxious to bring this request to an already overloaded staff member.

We decided it would be best to bring the question—not the answer—back to the faculty and see what would emerge in discussion. As with any group of teachers working together for many years, we were not totally surprised to find the larger group faculty discussion was almost identical to our previous conversation. We all seemed to land on the idea of the Library/Resource Center, much to the chagrin of our Resource Center director. But good sport that she is, she quickly assessed the need for additional shelving.

Concerns emerged for the privacy of children. Would students look at other children's portfolios? Of more concern was whether parents would examine the portfolios of children other than their own. Who would watch? I recognized these unanswerable fears as the plague of all forward movement. Lacking confidence in the final product, we are often unwilling to take the required risks—risks that in the end turn out to be a source of comfort and affirmation. Somehow, we got through that discussion, and although acknowledging these concerns as real, we decided to move the portfolio archives to the Resource Center.

Further reflections and hallway conversations elaborated on our initial plan. If we were to have an Archive, why not make it a School Archive, not just a place for portfolios? On its fiftieth anniversary, our school building was designated a national historic landmark. The innovative design and architecture of our school building, coupled with the developmental philosophy of the district in place prior to the building of Crow Island, has been the subject of numerous journal articles, texts, and books devoted to cutting-edge ideas in education. These photos and publications could be given a special place in our archive. One of the unique qualities of the community of Winnetka is its strong commitment to the schools. In fact, an unusual number of our students' parents were themselves students in our schools. How our students enjoy seeing their parents' faces included in old class pictures—some with their current teacher! We decided to include those many binders of classroom photos. As already noted, on the occasion of our school's fiftieth anniversary, we sent out an alumni question-naire to hundreds of former students asking them to share their most significant memories of their elementary school years. The letters we received in response are kept in the archive so that children can learn from these former students' memories.

So we went about the work of gathering all these photos and articles and books as well as making decisions about how the student portfolios would be organized. At first we assumed we would arrange the portfolios by grade level and classroom. Thinking further, it occurred to us that it would be impossible to locate a child's archive without knowing that child's grade level and current teacher. Our Resource Center director reminded us of the yearly task of reshelving the archival envelopes as children progressed through the grade levels and into different classrooms. A wiser solution was to shelve the archives alphabetically. More important than resolving the ready access problem, the alphabetized shelving resonated beautifully with an important archival message to children. You are not just a student in Mrs. Smith's classroom—you are a part of Crow Island School, its significant history, and the memories of generations of former students. Your archive will be placed in approximately the same location as long as you are a student here. Your archive will be shelved right next to those of your brothers and sisters, thus reinforcing the metaphor of family and school.

Students periodically examine their archive and relate the contents to current projects. When they complete their elementary years at Crow Island, the archives are given to each child. Identifying the Archive as the place containing our history was an important step in our project. It serves as a tangible reminder that we are all linked together through the history of our school and that our individual stories occur within the context of a larger human story. The Archive is a concrete symbol of inclusiveness, reminding students that everyone in the school is represented with an equal but unique voice. The establishment of our Archive added a sense of history to the portfolio. The predictable location, accessibility, and the inclusion of documents of each child and the whole school's history all resonate with values familiar and important to children.

This notion of an archive worked for us; that is, we found it useful and congenial to keep current students' portfolios as well as a repository for our school's historical documents, class pictures and other photos, alumni recollections, books, and articles about our landmark school. However, the realities of available space in schools may differ significantly. In response, there are many adjustments that can be made. The size of the portfolio archive, that is, the number of items selected to be retained, could be limited so as to make efficient use of available space within the school. If space is not available in the school for an all-school Archive, other sites within the community could be considered, for example, community centers, recreation centers, libraries, or historical museums. Although we return the children's archives to them when they leave our school, there are other ways of thinking about these personal histories. In some communities, it might be possible to store selections from children's archives. When she critiqued the manuscript for this book, writer Penelope Mesic came up with a charming insight: "Consider the value of discovering the school work, artwork, and reflections of hundreds of children during the Civil War, the Great Depression, or other significant times in our history. Imagine what a community resource these might be to future generations." We could learn a great deal about education and culture from such rich records!

Now that we had secured a place for these memories, we pursued faculty discussions about specifying an audience and creating an event when children could present their portfolios. Establishing an authentic audience is fundamental to the purpose of maintaining portfolios. The notion of gathering work to tell a story is far too abstract unless children know there is someone listening. For our students, the parents were the most natural audience. Other audiences to be considered are siblings, older or younger students in the school, prior teachers in the school, peer-level classrooms of students, or senior citizens in the community.

Learning is a celebratory event. Once we specified the audience, we sought a unifying experience that would consolidate all of our discussions and concerns; an event for the children and parents that would clearly communicate the value portfolios held for us. We decided that child-led evening conferences with parents were compatible with all of our goals. Children love being in charge and so we were confident that a Portfolio Conference Evening would be very appealing to our students.

Reflection Tag

I chose this piece for my portfolio because . . .

It explains how Portfolio Conferences brought it all together for us. Celebrating learning, specifying a particular audience for the children, and creating an Archive were among the best ideas we had. Children delighted in the special responsibility the conferences bestowed upon them.

LESSON 8

A Celebration Connects Child, Portfolio, and Audience

"C'mon, we'll be late!" urged one second grader tugging at her mother's wrist. The teachers and I stood outside the classrooms in nervous anticipation of this evening's event. We were confident in our belief in children's ability to take a lead role in a conference with their parents, but we didn't know how parents would react to this change in our conference format. As a procession of moms and dads and children were entering the school we were wondering if our students would be able to fulfill such a huge responsibility. We were out on a limb, and we knew it.

Traditional parent-teacher conferences are fraught with tensions on both sides. We hoped that the plan we had come up with for this evening would replace one of those regularly scheduled, adult transactions when the child is discussed but not seen or heard. But would parents attribute importance to a conference managed by their child and not the teacher? Would parents understand that this carefully organized conversation with their son or daughter could have long-term significance for that child as a learner? It was an ideal opportunity both for children to have the importance of their learning acknowledged and for parents to learn about our attempts to help their children achieve genuine understanding about themselves as learners and as people. But would it be perceived that way? Just before the first student arrived, the teachers and I nervously eyed each other. With that exchange of glances we acknowledged that either we were on to something very important or we could be making a huge mistake.

Many children arrived earlier than the scheduled 7 P.M. start, hurriedly making their way to their classrooms. None of us had given any instructions about dress and yet, one after another, the children arriving were dressed up! Boys' seldom-seen foreheads were visible, a clear sign that they had combed their hair. Girls had cast off their uniform of jeans and sweats—they were wearing dresses! Who told them to dress up for Portfolio Evening? What to wear had never come up in our faculty discussions. This was the signal we were waiting for. Of course—they had told themselves how to dress because tonight was their special evening: the very first Portfolio Conference Evening at Crow Island School. As we witnessed this parade of neatly attired, confident children, we again flashed glances at each other, this time with reassuring smiles. No doubt about it, we were on to something very important!

Before we move to the children's encounters with parents, it's important to explain how portfolio conferences are organized. To prepare for this event, the children spend several weeks in conversations about their portfolio archive with their teacher, with peers, and sometimes with older students as well. Specific lessons are focused on how to organize selections and how to place them in chronological order, how to think about their work as evidence of competence in more than one subject area, how to make comparisons of prior work with present work including more advanced skills, and, most important, how to reflect upon this work as a whole. Guiding questions that structure the conversations include

- How has your writing changed since last year (or since September)?
- What do you know about numbers now that you didn't know in the beginning of the year?
- Let's compare a page from a book you were reading last year and a book you are reading now and include copies of each in your portfolio.

- What is unique about your portfolio?
- What would you like Mom and Dad to understand about your portfolio? Can you organize it so it will show that?

Such guiding questions and thoughtful responses to the answers help children reflect on their learning. As children review their work, they complete reflection tags and attach them to specific pieces of work they find noteworthy. The preparation to explain their story to their parents allows the children to organize and clarify for themselves the essential features of the narrative they want to relate. Most students complete an organizational form or a portfolio menu, often called an "Ask me about" sheet. On these organizing sheets the students highlight some of the contents of their portfolio that reflect learning experiences that are important to their portfolio story. For example:

ASK ME ABOUT . . .
- Coins
- My job
- Books I've read
- My writing folder
- My fourth grade buddy
- My baby chicks journal
- My locker

     —*Martha, first grade*

These organizing sheets serve as a to-do list and act as a reminder of particular aspects of a child's school life to which they attribute importance. Teachers stimulate this reflective process by providing guidelines and helping to structure the child's thinking in an evaluative mode: "What is the process we use for learning spelling?" "Review the goals you wrote in September. . . . Which goals have been completed? Which goals are you still working on?" "Can you explain to your parents how you add fractions?"

Getting Ready for Portfolio Evening

Throughout the fall and early winter the students have experienced a wide variety of portfolio conversations, lessons, and activities incorporated into the classroom curriculum. As the dates for their grade-level Portfolio Conference Evenings approach (in either February, March, or May) more time is allotted to organizing the current year's portfolio, reexamining the archive, and preparing for the conference.

Students are taken to the Crow Island Archive in our Library/Resource Center to retrieve their personal archive—their collection of past years' portfolios—and return with them to their classroom. This is a magical day for students. The students are so pleased that evidence of their personal school history has been safely maintained for them.

As they return to their classrooms each student finds an area of the room to reexamine and rediscover the contents they have selected over the years. The room is filled with generous laughter and disbelief as well as feelings of satisfaction. Third grade students often shake their heads as they attempt to reread stories written in first grade. Although recognizing the story as their own they are often unable to decipher the invented phonetic spelling that accompanied their drawings. One student ponders a sketch of a horse she made two years ago. She sits on the rug examining and remembering this single artifact as she holds it in her hand. After some moments, and as if just rediscovering her genuine interest in horses, she announces to a nearby classmate that she intends to use that drawing for her upcoming animal report. The connection between prior interests and present ideas and projects is ideally supported with a portfolio.

Over a period of weeks the children rehearse the sequence of their portfolio story with a teacher or a classmate or an older student who knows the younger child in a "learning buddy" relationship. Children are naturally inclined to the authentic task of telling the story of how they learn. Most demonstrate a heightened focus and attention not always present in subject area lessons they don't conceive of as their own. They are aware of their own competence in fulfilling the obligations of this important work and they are anxious to demonstrate their worthiness for the trust their teacher has placed in them.

In the days just prior to the evening, the children add final touches to their presentations. Each child selects an area of the classroom where they can be seated to have a private conversation with their parents. The teacher adds welcoming words on the blackboard as well as a few reminders for students.

Inviting Parents to Portfolio Evening

Parents are invited to the Portfolio Evening by a letter from the teacher, often followed by a letter or reminder from the child as well. Mailing a letter to parents that outlines the purposes and expectations of the Portfolio Conference is another way of attributing importance to the event (see sample letter on p. 91). The dates of these evenings have been included on the school calendar at the beginning the year. Second and third grade students hold their Portfolio Conference Evenings in February or March. First, fourth, and fifth grade students schedule their Portfolio Conferences later in the spring. We chose these different times of the year because some grade levels benefit from a mid-year celebratory event that renews learning goals for the year. Teachers of older students felt that the Portfolio Conference Evening best coincided with year-end events and culminating activities. First grade teachers did not hold Portfolio Evenings for the first few years because they were uncertain whether our youngest full-day students could benefit from this event. But once one first grade teacher ventured into a Portfolio Conference Evening with her students, the good news traveled fast! We were thrilled to find out that our first graders eagerly and competently fulfilled their responsibilities.

In addition to satisfying different grade-level expectations, it was prudent to separate the events by the space of a few months so that parents with more than one child in the school would find no difficulty in attending multiple conferences. In grades one through three half of the class attends one night and the other half on the following night so there's ample space for the assembled parents and children. Each evening lasts approximately ninety minutes. In grades four and five two sessions are held on a single evening.

On the following page is a sample letter that explains Portfolio Conference Evening to parents.

Portfolio Evening Arrives

It is twelve years since we first started holding Portfolio Conferences but students continue to arrive in the same manner, that is, early and dressed for a special event. As the children come in, they take their parents' coats (in cooler weather) and hang them in their own lockers. The students enter the classroom with independence, focus, and a real job to accomplish. They lead their parents to the private area of the classroom that they have designated for their conference. Without any direction from their teacher they begin their work, each in a different way. The teacher is present to welcome the families, to help students get started when needed, and to monitor the schedule for the evening. The students begin the evening by presenting their portfolios to their parents. Many children love to begin with a review of their earliest learning in Kindergarten and then slowly move through the years to the present. Other students will focus on the present year's portfolio and, as time allows, select highlights of their archive from prior years. All of these decisions and variations are influenced by the particulars of the process used in that classroom, that year, and with that teacher, as well as by each child's different experiences of that same process in prior years. These variations are not at all troublesome to children. They appreciate the diverse ways in which meaning can be constructed out of learning.

Each child will review their portfolio archive in a way that satisfies their concept of the right way to tell their parents the story of what they have learned. Crow Island teachers have discovered it is best not to impose a rigid standard of correctness on this portfolio conversation because we recognize that the diverse ways in which

Sample Parent Letter of Invitation to Portfolio Evening

Dear Parents of First Grade Students,

As many of you know, the use of portfolios as a major tool for observing and reflecting on children's growth at school has become a rich part of life at Crow Island. Starting in Kindergarten, children collect items that tell a story about themselves as learners. Each one-year collection stays at school as the children progress through the grades and the collection of portfolios becomes an Archive, traveling on with each child.

The portfolio is a powerful tool for the child, but also for the teacher and parent as well. It allows all of us to see in a dramatic way the progress children make over time. Children delight in poring through work done in previous years, exclaiming, "Wow, I can't believe I got that wrong! . . . That is so easy for me now!" "Look how I spelled that word!" and "Oh, I remember when I did that painting!" These observations and self-evaluation by the young child are important steps toward a student's sense of ownership and commitment to the tasks of school.

At Crow Island, we have come to understand how valuable it is for children not only to have access to their work over time, but also for them to share their reflections with the primary adults in their lives. Thus, the Portfolio Evening Conference, an evening meeting where children are the expert presenters of their lives at school and the work they do here, is a time for each child to tell his or her parents about school. And it is a chance for parents to listen uninterrupted to their child as they begin to make connections between the work of school and their own sense of growth.

I am really looking forward to this adventure, and I am sure that with your collaboration it will be an outstanding experience for all of us, but most notably for your children.

Sincerely,

Eva Tarini
First Grade Teacher

NAME _____

Parents, please check the nights you are available:

_____ Wednesday, May 22   _____ Thursday, May 23

PLEASE RETURN BY FRIDAY. I WILL SEND ASSIGNMENTS NOTES ASAP. THANKS!

children think about their own learning over time is reflected in their choices and each method has validity.

First graders are thrilled with this new responsibility bestowed upon them. They take it very seriously. Catherine holds her red portfolio folder on her lap. Her parents are seated very close to her on either side. She pulls out her Science Journal and places it on her desk. "This is my chick diary. When they're five days old this is what they look like." She looks to both parents' faces for a response. "I didn't know that," says her dad, acknowledging for Catherine that she has taught him something new.

Being in charge of the conference is very important to second graders. Billy has selected items from his yellow portfolio folder and placed them on his desk. His dad is anxious about getting started. He asks Billy, "So how do we do this? Should I ask you about this?" "No, not yet—I'll show you," responds Billy, still organizing his work on his desk. Billy highlights a story he has written and presented at Author's Chair. He then selects his math book and turns to a premarked page with multiplication problems. His science journal with drawings of plants at different stages is Billy's next focus. With each piece of work, Billy reads the accompanying reflection tag to his dad and notes particular pieces of work that were hard for him. As Billy gains his own rhythm for presenting his portfolio, his dad senses that Billy really does know how to do a portfolio conference. "You know what?—I'm really proud of you," he tells his son.

By third grade, students competently review their portfolios for their parents. They point out differences in their reading and writing skills that have evolved over these past few months of third grade. Schoolwork has become more difficult and third graders want mom and dad to know that. Olivia sorts the contents of her portfolio into neat piles on top of her desk. "Here's my math book. You have to know how to multiply and to keep your numbers lined up," she notes. "Wow! That's a lot of work," her mom responds.

Fourth graders typically focus on the amount and variety of work they complete. Madeline opens her art portfolio. She takes some time to talk about one of her watercolors. Her eyes never leave the work as she describes in great detail the dry brush technique she used and how she layered the water color washes for the seascape. "I worked hard on this," she comments to her parents. "May I have that for my office?" asks her dad.

Fifth graders love to show the multiple drafts of stories they have kept as part of their portfolio. It proves how hard they have worked and that learning is not easy. "OK. Look at this. This is cool. Here's a story I wrote in first grade and here's my Research Report," notes Matthew. He points out to his mom—and himself—that more is expected of you when you're in fifth grade. "I can see you have been working very hard," his mom responds.

Listening and waiting for your child to show you what they've learned is not always easy advice to follow. It's important for teachers to know that not all parents agree with the idea of a child leading the conference. In those instances, it's important for the teacher to be close by to support the child and offer any information that will clarify the child's presentation.

Zach is in second grade. He has collected samples of his writing that are important to him. He includes his writing journal that contains a riddle he wrote. He wants to share it with his mom. Zach's mom is troubled by the misspellings and she continues to leaf through the journal asking him why his teacher hasn't checked it. Zach's teacher, seeing the disappointment on his face, approaches and reminds Zach's mom that entries in the journal are not given a final edit as this particular journal is a child's own collection of process writing. She asks Zach, "Can you show your mom one of your stories that you edited for spelling?" Zach has no problem retrieving an edited story that, although well written, is not one of his favorites. "Can I read my riddle now?" he asks. Reassured by the evidence of her son's spelling skills, Zach's mom gives him a hug and responds, "Yes, I'd love to hear your riddle."

At all grade levels the sequence of the evening is the same. After spending approximately forty-five minutes reviewing their portfolio and touring their parents around exhibits in the classroom, everyone gathers on the rug to view the classroom video portfolio.

The Classroom Portfolio: A Collaborative Video Project

In addition to children's individual stories of learning, each classroom experiences a collective learning story that is important to relate. The production of a classroom videotape is yet another dimension of portfolio development. This video is intended to portray a day in the life of this particular group of students, including the learning that takes place in special subject areas of Art, Music, Physical Education, Spanish, and Library/Technology. Many classroom videotapes also include recess activities and selected field trips. Approximately twenty minutes in length, the videotape is an important collaborative segment of the Portfolio Conference celebration.

The organization, scripting, and filming of this videotape is a multifaceted task that the children look forward to eagerly. Reviewing and reflecting upon the routines, rituals, and projects associated with the school day, children select the scenes, the sequence, and the words to describe their group learning experiences. Each student is responsible for introducing some aspect of the school day and writing the script for that segment of the video. These planning conversations allow students to be influenced by each other's levels of thinking as they compose meaningful verbal explanations in connection with the learning experiences of the school day.

"Hola! Have you ever tasted guacamole? Come join us in Spanish and you'll learn the word for taste." "Hi, I'm Caroline and on Tuesdays, we go to Library. We are learning about how books are organized in the library. Come join us." "Hi, my name is Bradley. Every day we do mental math. That's math you do in your head without pencil and paper."

In recent years, many groups of students have adopted a news anchor show format and assigned each other roving reporter assignments to describe their school day news to parents.

"Good evening. Welcome to Second Grade Ng News and I'm Kevin. It's been a busy school day in Mrs. Ng's classroom. What's been going on out on the playground, Patrick?"

"Hi, I'm Patrick. . . . We're out here on the playground—the girls are playing four square and the boys play in the woods. . . . It's a lot of fun! Back to you Kevin."

Older students incorporate advanced technical highlights into the video, that acknowledge their interest and competence in this technological area. Extensive use of fade-ins and explosive and colorful images as well as musical accompaniment will be found in many fourth and fifth grade classroom video portfolios.

The production of the videotape serves another purpose as well, that is, the gradual transition of ownership of the portfolio experience from teacher to child. Our first videotapes were produced through the teacher lens. Our purpose was to provide parents with information about their child's typical school day including the many special subject classrooms that comprise a comprehensive curricular experience for all children. Over time, we were able to share and even give control to the students for the decisions about organizing this project. We found that the children view the curriculum through a different lens. In addition to the subject area experiences that the teacher would highlight, children consider the playground, lunchroom, and student council meetings as equally significant experiences in their learning.

In producing the classroom video, the fundamental task always remains the same. Given an authentic project, children reflect on their school experience and attach words and hence meaning to their learning. The ongoing rehearsal of the metacognitive task serves the essential purposes of maintaining a portfolio, that is, to connect prior and present learning, to solidify self-insights about the process of learning, and to make broader and more relevant connections between various learning experiences.

The process of compiling portfolios, and especially the event of Portfolio Evenings, has provided our students with an authentic sense of control of their evaluation. Children derive a personal sense of achievement as their parents and teachers support their investigation of learning with direction and encouragement. The essential elements are really two—the notion of celebration and the specified audience. Although the evening schedule worked well for our purposes, the portfolio conference can take place before, during, or after school. The important thing is for children to have a specific audience for the celebration. As I noted earlier, if parents are not available, other audiences could include older brothers and sisters, grandparents, older students in the school, prior teachers of these students, or local senior center groups.

Year after year, we observe this ritual progress in remarkably similar ways. Regardless of the age of the child, the newness of the teacher, or the time of year, children eagerly and readily assume the responsibility for talking about their learning. In recording their thoughts about the evening, even young students recognize their responsible role in the conference and gain confidence as they realize what they have achieved. Younger students, especially, tell us that they value direct involvement in their assessment: "I liked being in charge." "Mom and Dad asked *me* questions about my work instead of asking my teacher."

Reflection Tag

I chose this piece for my portfolio because . . .

We shouldn't forget that we need to teach parents how to listen to their child's portfolio presentation—this is a very new experience for them. Each year a group of our teachers meets with parents to share their insights and experiences with portfolios. A serendipitous by-product of this gathering is how it energizes the group. Prideful association with the wise words of colleagues is an unstated but invaluable gift we provide to each other.

LESSON 9

Teaching Parents How to Be Part of the Portfolio Conference

In a classroom of anxious parents sitting with their eager first graders, Jessie and her younger brother were easy to spot. Jessie (an eighth grader) was less than half these parents' age but she had twice their confidence. Her face shone with inside knowledge as she listened to her brother comparing early journal writing samples with a newer story. He proudly pointed out the differences between his large printing in the fall and his more recently acquired ability to refine the movements of his pencil and transfer his thoughts into writing. She looked equally attentively at his Polaroid photographs of recess games, which prompted a conversation about developing friendships—an important dimension of the first grade experience.

Jessie was not at all anxious about fulfilling her responsibilities that evening because she knew what to do. She listened and she waited to be shown what her brother had prepared. Not so long ago, she had taught their parents how to listen to her own portfolio presentation. Now an eighth grader just two weeks away from graduation, Jessie was her brother's audience for this special evening. The parents of the other children in the classroom gazed at this lovely adolescent girl, admiring both her youthful poise and her obvious competence for the task at hand. Not all parents come into the room sure of how they were meant to listen and respond. Jessie was a model of correct behavior for parents experiencing their first Portfolio Conference Evening at Crow Island School.

We had spent years training the children how to ask themselves questions that would help them organize and present their portfolio. But we soon realized that we had unintentionally left the task of educating the parents to the children. And although there is value in that source of instruction, we decided that a direct teacher presentation to parents was in order.

In the first years of Portfolio Conferences at Crow Island, parents were unsure of their role. The idea of sitting down with your child—not the teacher—and listening to your child's account of the year's learning is a new experience for most parents. They need direction as well as encouragement to understand their child's unique portfolio presentation. Now, with the confidence and experience of many years, we are able to provide the appropriate structure for the parents to genuinely *hear* their child's portfolio presentation and gain a more in-depth view of their child as a learner.

As a faculty, we wanted parents to know what portfolios meant to us. We wanted them to see how we use them as a part of our curriculum and their immeasurable value to the children. We hoped they'd understand how they fit into an assessment program for our school. We needed to emphasize that portfolios do not replace standardized measures. As noted in an earlier chapter, standardized tests address the question "Which child knows *more?*" and portfolios address the question "What does *this* child know?" One question is not better than the other—posing both questions will provide a more comprehensive perspective of a child's work in school.

Planning a Meeting for Parents

We began, as we always do, by having a planning conversation. A group of interested teachers met to discuss the possible content and format for a meeting with parents about portfolios. How could we best communicate our experiences and convictions about portfolios and distill our insights into a meaningful, instructive statement to parents? After considering the important aspects of portfolio, our group finally decided that the idea of the portfolio over time was probably the most useful concept for parents. We wanted to show that the portfolio develops as time passes and that the skills, content, and ways of understanding the portfolio grow with the child as learning strategies develop.

Along with that goal we wanted parents to understand that each child's portfolio could have a different content. We wanted parents to know that teachers have different understandings of the portfolio concept and that each teacher's perspective would shape their child's portfolio for any given year. Most important, we wanted parents to understand what they should do at this conference. Learning to listen and waiting to be shown by the child are essential skills for a Portfolio Conference hosted by a child.

We decided that we would form a panel of teachers, one from each grade level. This format would best communicate the portfolio over time. In addition, the parents would have an opportunity to overhear good collegial conversation from a group of teachers in their child's school. For the past seven years now, a panel of teachers has presented this informational program for our parents. Our first meeting to inform parents about portfolios was held during the school day, but we quickly concluded that more parents would be available in the evening. We included notice of the meeting in our weekly school *Bulletin* sent home to parents:

FACULTY PORTFOLIO PANEL

An important part of a child's learning at Crow Island is the ongoing compilation of a portfolio and the annual sharing of portfolios on Portfolio Evenings. The collaboration of children, parents, and teachers in this process is vital to the success of instructing students how to participate in understanding and assessing their own learning. One of the goals of our current Crow Island Annual Plan is to continue the parent education sessions to prepare parents for their role in the Portfolio Evening Process.

Please join us on Tuesday, January 18, at 7 P.M. for a discussion about the purposes and diversity of our students' portfolios. The program offers another perspective on student assessment to supplement earlier presentations on our School Improvement Plan and Standardized Testing. [Names of teachers and their grade levels] and I will be sharing our perspectives and experiences with portfolios. We look forward to meeting with you on the evening of January 18th.

Usually I begin the meeting with an overview of our experience with portfolios. I explain that our main purpose is to support all the children as competent participants in the assessment of their own learning. I differentiate this evening's gathering from an earlier annual meeting focused on test scores. I note that both ways of viewing a child's learning are valuable.

Following these initial remarks, each teacher speaks for about three or four minutes about the value and purposes of portfolio for children at a particular grade level. Over the years, these individual presentations have varied as different teachers join the panel and share anecdotes of children's experiences or examples of classroom discussions to illuminate the child's view of the process at each grade level.

In an attempt to make our message more concrete, each year—with the child's permission—we borrow one fifth grader's archive for the evening, promising, of course, not to reveal any of the specific contents. Right before the meeting we distribute the individual portfolio envelopes from this archive to each of the teachers on the panel.

The Kindergarten teacher holds the manila Kindergarten portfolio folder while speaking to the parents about the very beginnings of the portfolio experience and explaining how the ideas of making choices, collecting work over time, and keeping some work at school in a special place are introduced to Kindergartners. At the end, the Kindergarten teacher places the manila folder in the red-roped archival envelope and passes it on to the first grade teacher, who is already holding up the red first grade portfolio folder.

The teacher explains that first graders may have heard about portfolios and Portfolio Evenings from their older brothers and sisters. Young children love the idea of making decisions about what to save. They are prompted to think about the reasons these pieces of work are important to them. These reflections are dictated to a teacher or a fifth grade "learning buddy." At the conclusion of these remarks, the first grade teacher places the red portfolio in the archival envelope and passes it on.

The second grade teacher holds up the yellow second grade portfolio, outlining the competencies and developmental milestones of the seven-year-old student with regard to portfolio organization and presentation. Second graders, their teacher explains, make more decisions. They now have the responsibility of writing their own reflection tags. The spoken language of the seven-year-old is far more sophisticated than their written language skills and so the challenge of recording their thoughts on reflection tags is considerable. Another sophisticated task is making decisions about the script of the classroom videotape. The planning and filming of this project is an opportunity for the students to take the lead—a subtle exchange of roles for teacher and student.

The third grade teacher holds up the blue portfolio folder and reminds the parent audience that when third graders visit the Archive in the Library/Resource Center, they are very aware of the place where the history of their learning is maintained. With two years of portfolio conferences under their belts, third graders approach the organization of their portfolio with a high degree of competence and confidence. Students in third grade are given the opportunity to make more decisions about how to organize their portfolio content—chronologically, or by interest, or by favorites. At this age, children show they realize that their peers experience this same process. Their sensitivity to the differences in each other's portfolio collections is developing.

A team of fourth grade teachers then hold up the green portfolio container. They speak to the ways in which the portfolio is enhanced through video images, an illustration of how one teacher conceptualizes the portfolio journey. Children review video clips that chronicle their learning activities. This grounds the portfolio process in the curriculum. The teachers remind parents to let their child lead the conference on Portfolio Evening. They emphasize that "listening for your child's meaning" and "waiting to be shown" are critical.

Accepting the nearly full archival envelope, the fifth grade teacher remarks on the fifth grade student's experience in organizing the entire archive, and adds the fifth grade choice of a black binder. As these oldest students examine their collections, they reflect on their entire elementary school experience. At the close of the fifth grade year, the teacher explains, the archives are given to our students who will begin their next school year in the middle school.

Fitting Portfolios into a School's Assessment Program

Talking to parents about the portfolio experience is very important to us. It is, however, only one strand of a more comprehensive program of educating parents about their child's progress in school. In December of each year, prior to our Portfolio Panel, I meet with parents to present our students' performance on standardized measures of achievement that were administered the prior year. Parents are invited to this meeting with an announcement in the weekly *Bulletin*:

> *Talking About Tests:* Please join me on Wednesday, December 6th, at 7:00 P.M. in the Crow Island Foyer for our annual presentation and discussion about standardized testing. Results of the ISAT (Illinois Standards Achievement Tests) over the last few years, together with the CAT (California Achievement Test) scores will be reviewed. A longitudinal analysis of Crow Island's performance on standardized tests will be presented.

The format of this meeting is quite different from our Portfolio Panel—as it should be. I present a series of overheads that illustrate our students' most recent test scores as well as consolidated data that demonstrate trends in our school's scores over the last few years.

In addition to this meeting, and in compliance with our state's Assessment Plan for all public schools, we prepare an *Annual Report* that functions as an audit of our school's performance on stated goals. This thirty-five-page detailed document serves to educate parents about our school's programs and practices. A summary of this report is presented at one of our monthly Board of Education meetings. The following excerpts from our school's *Annual Report* focus specifically on our assessment program and our multiple vehicles for communication between the home and school.

ASSESSMENT SYSTEM AND STUDENT WORK

Assessment and evaluation of children's learning is an ongoing process and an integral part of our instructional program. Close, careful, and collaborative observation of children over time is a fundamental part of our program. In addition to these observations, we utilize a number of assessment tools to gain a fuller understanding of how children learn. More standardized measures are introduced at Grades 3, 4 & 5 with the Illinois Standards Achievement Test (ISAT) and the California Achievement Tests (CAT), which are used to augment our assessment program.

Portfolios, thoughtful collections of student work over time, are an important part of the culture of Crow Island School. We've been growing in our understandings of the uses of portfolios with our students for the past fourteen years. We believe that portfolios tell a child's story of learning and that the specific contents of the collection are far less important than the thoughtful process that children engage in as they construct and assess collections of their work over time. We have learned that a child's understanding of portfolio becomes embedded in their learning as we provide more opportunities for them to be "in charge" and articulate the linkages between prior and present learning. Portfolio Evenings are an opportunity for parents to participate in this important part of the child's learning.

Newsletters from teacher to parents reinforce curricular goals and objectives and provide specific information about a child's school day. The purpose of these letters is not only to provide information but also to encourage parent participation in the process of their child's learning and to develop a greater understanding between the school and family.

Curriculum Overviews, that is, descriptions of the district wide instructional program, provide parents with a broad scope and sequence of the curriculum for the child's grade level.

HOME–SCHOOL COMMUNICATION

The value of a child-centered philosophy of instruction requires communication between home and school to highlight areas of emphasis that exemplify our mutual goals. The following events, documents, and practices are only a partial listing of the value we place on communication with parents:

- *Go To School Nights:* Fall open house when the teacher's instructional program for the year is presented to parents.

- *Regularly scheduled parent conferences* in Fall and Winter and an optional conference in Spring.

- *Written Learning Experience Forms* are provided for parents at the end of the year as a review of student work in all areas. In the Fall parents complete a Reflection sheet that serves as the focus of the October conference.

- *Portfolio Evening Conferences* are a time for children to present a collection of their own work to their parents and take part in the evaluation of their learning.

- *Telephones:* in each classroom/office in order to facilitate school-home communication.

- *Weekly Bulletin:* organized by the PTA, where events of the school are announced.

- *Classroom newsletters* inform parents of curricular activities and upcoming events.

- *Specials Newsletter:* occasional publication informing parents of curricular themes and activities in Music, Art, Kinetic Wellness, Spanish & Technology.

- *Reflections: Teachers & Parents:* a column in the weekly *Bulletin* for teachers and parents to contribute a written selection for publication with their reflections on teaching and learning.

- *School Directory:* a publication of the PTA providing general information about the school as well as an alphabetized listing of all students, families and faculty.

- *Regularly scheduled daytime and evening PTA meetings:* when issues and programs are discussed.

- *End-of-year letters from parents to Principal* provide an opportunity for parents to evaluate the current year and help the school plan for the following year for each child. A letter is sent home to parents inviting this end-of-year reflection.

Each year we consider school goals in addition to our district's goals. In our statements of progress we focus attention on specific building initiatives or programs. We include our Portfolio Program in our goals as an important component of assessment as well as parent education.

BUILDING GOALS FOR CROW ISLAND

- *To continue to refine our communication to parents so that they are well informed about their child's progress as it relates to past school performance and future goals. In addition, parents should understand their youngster's progress, within the context of the individual classroom, the school, and the community, as well as on state and national standardized measures. Parent education sessions will continue to prepare parents for their role in the Portfolio Evening Process. Additional meetings and written information will inform parents about the measures of assessment and evaluation of student performance used at Crow Island.*

Last year our faculty conducted over 1200 formal conferences with parents about their child's progress. These meetings include regularly scheduled parent conferences, special education staffings and IEP Annual reviews and other scheduled meetings as needed to plan for a child's successful school year. In addition, countless "informal" conferences and phone calls help parents and teachers stay in touch to coordinate and revise student programs. Last year all schools in the district invited parents to share their thoughts about the coming school year in written form. Parent Reflection Forms were distributed to all parents on Go To School Night and parents devoted considerable time and thoughtfulness in communicating information about their child that gave additional structure to our fall parent conferences.

In frequent faculty meetings and articulation meetings, our faculty discussed the purpose and content of conferences with parents. Providing meaningful information in a format that can be easily understood by parents has been our goal. Feedback from parents as contained in end-of-the-year letters to the Principal indicate that we were successful in those efforts.

Parent meetings were held in December and January to review our students' performance on the Illinois Goals Assessment Program (IGAP) and the California Achievement Test. These meetings reviewed the most current scores as well as trends over the past ten years.

In addition to the standardized measures of evaluation used at Crow Island, all of our students maintain a portfolio of samples of their work. Direct involvement of students in the assessment of their learning is an important part of the culture at Crow Island. On one evening in the year, the children are given the responsibility to present their portfolios individually to their parents and to explain to them the process by which the materials had been generated, the self-reflections the process involved, the conversations with the teacher that had spurred particular selections to be made and any other aspects of their learning story they want to share.

Teaching parents about the process their children go through in compiling their portfolios is an important part of our parent education program. Each January a panel of faculty share their grade-level approaches to the introduction and development of assisting students with this crucial task. Last January this meeting was well attended.

Classroom teachers provide extensive written communication in the form of newsletters, notes and updates about current units of instruction, homework assignments as well as explanations regarding current lessons. In addition, our "Specials Teachers" (Music, Strings, Band, Art, Kinetic Wellness, Spanish, & Technology) collaborated on a series of newsletters that informed parents about the specific curricular events in these classes that are part of each child's instructional program [excerpt from *Annual Plan*].

Educating parents about the many ways that a child's learning can be measured and understood is an important goal for any school. As parents learn more about multiple tools for assessment they will become better able to understand the different kinds of information that each process yields.

Reflection Tag

I chose this piece for my portfolio because . . .

Laurie's story takes the portfolio concept to another level. She showed me new dimensions of the portfolio. Children who have experienced organizing and reflecting on the contents of their portfolio over time have many lessons to teach us. We're really still at the very beginning of understanding what a portfolio can be.

LESSON 10

Listening for Children's Meaning

Ten-year-old Laurie and I were exhilarated by the possibilities that lay before us, although we were uncertain how to begin. The contents of her six-year archive were spread out on the table. We had a task to complete and a deadline drawing near. The task for Laurie was to present her archive to a group of thirty visiting teachers she had never seen before. My task was to assist Laurie and to test that fundamental principle of portfolios—child ownership. The deadline was tomorrow at 1:30. As we prepared to work together, each with different purposes, we giggled nervously and tried to convince each other that we knew what we were doing.

And of course we did know what we were doing. Laurie had reviewed her archive countless times over the years. As principal of a school where student portfolios have been developing for over a dozen years, I have addressed hundreds of teachers and written numerous articles about organizing student portfolios. Surely, we could draw on this expertise for this task. But this was different. The context was going to change; the audience would not be mom and dad; the language would need to be different. Our many years of accumulated knowledge about portfolios was about to be challenged.

Affirming Child Ownership

The day before, a quick glance at my calendar had reminded me that a group of teachers from the Chicago Public Schools would be visiting to learn about our portfolio project. The normal chaotic events of the past few school days had filled my mental spaces, and I was not as prepared as I should have been. I wanted to crystallize our project for these teachers. As a former Chicago Public Schools teacher, I continue to feel a tinge of defensiveness about having spent the last seventeen years of my professional career in an affluent North Shore suburb. I needed to transcend the urban-suburban divide and select the most essential and universal attributes of portfolios, the ones that would remain authentic in any school.

Thinking about what to present to the visiting teachers, I stopped in a first grade classroom where the teacher was reading a favorite book to her students. And as the children recited the recurrent rhythmic phrase of this much-loved children's book, it all began to come together for me. "But the most important thing about a chair is that you sit on it . . . and the most important thing about a book is that you read it." And the most important thing about portfolios, I thought, is that children do them.

Momentarily enlightened by this most fundamental premise of our project, I needed to figure out how to make this truth evident to our teacher visitors. I approached one of our fifth grade teachers and explained my dilemma. Could I borrow one of her fifth graders to speak to tomorrow's visiting group of teachers? Her students were busily working on their final Research Report. As we scanned the group we almost simultaneously decided that Laurie might enjoy the challenge of this project. She had an interpersonal sparkle—she was confident and friendly and interacted well with adults.

Her teacher beckoned her to the doorway and I asked Laurie if she would review her archive with me in front of thirty guest teachers! Excited about being selected for this special duty, and slightly overwhelmed, she looked to her teacher for permission and affirmation. Both were given to her with one encouraging nod. We arranged to meet that afternoon.

Until now, our students had been taught how to present their portfolios only to their parents. Early on we learned that defining an audience was crucial to the success and clarity of the task. Parents are a natural audience, and the conversation between parent and child is filled with unique understandings and language specific to that relationship. Could the child's understanding of portfolio be expressed to other audiences as well?

The first decision Laurie needed to make was how to select items from her archive across the years. Viewing children as competent and trusting the student to make meaningful decisions requires patience. This was Laurie's time to structure the conversation, so it was important not to impose my own expectation. I was careful not to say, for example, "Let's find your best narrative writing from second grade." Instead, we took each grade level portfolio individually and spread its contents out. I waited to see which two or three items her eyes went to and structured our conversation around those pieces.

Then we gathered her choices from her archive and made overheads of each artifact so that our audience could see them. The next afternoon after welcoming our visitors, we gathered in a classroom for Laurie's presentation. Here are excerpts from that conversation (with ellipses indicating pauses rather than omissions):

PRINCIPAL: How do you want to begin?

LAURIE: This is first grade. I enjoy writing a lot now. I did at other times. This piece is about friendship . . . that described friends and how you'd go down to the Library and check out books. I had a lot of friends then and I still have a lot of friends.

PRINCIPAL: Do you remember why you put this piece in your portfolio?

LAURIE: I was in Mrs. Kappos' class and she really made our minds think and there were no boundaries to our imagination. You could just think and put it on paper. This was one thing I really enjoyed doing. I could describe what I felt. I guess that's it, I thought this was a very good example to show how first graders write and how they can feel at times.

LAURIE: This is first grade memories. . . . This is me on Halloween. I was a pediatrician. I really enjoyed babies. You can see there's my doll . . . my favorite doll . . . I got it for Christmas . . . I used to bring it to school every day. I thought they were the most amazing things.

LAURIE: When I was at Lincoln Park Zoo I saw a picture of a Scientist, Farmer, and Business person. I put my face in the hole of the Scientist's face. I would pretend I was a Scientist or a Pediatrician or a very complicated thing. That was one of my favorite field trips.

LAURIE: (*from third grade portfolio*) This is my timeline . . . this is something I really remember making . . . this is my favorite time . . . when I was growing up . . . it reflects a lot on my athletic talents . . . I made the Trevian Soccer team . . . this timeline is something I'd like to continue.

LAURIE: (*from fourth grade portfolio*) This is reflective of my writing . . . this is the first time I'm getting very descriptive and I started putting a lot of time into my writing. That ending sentence was something I put in a poem I wrote in 3rd grade . . . one of my favorite endings.

LAURIE: (*from fifth grade portfolio*) This is recent work I'm doing. I'm doing my research report on premature babies.

I'm going to have a very detailed exhibit that will show how you feed them.

PRINCIPAL: What is it about this topic that interests you?

LAURIE: For me, as I said before in first grade, I was curious about being a pediatrician and nursing and just learning a lot about doctors and how they would take care of babies. . . . And now that I had an opportunity to go back and revise my stuff . . . I found out I was very interested in babies and I recall that interest from first grade.

PRINCIPAL: Will that affect some courses you take in high school?

LAURIE: Yes . . . I think I'm going to become a nurse or a teacher. If I become a teacher I'd like to learn more about this on the side.

PRINCIPAL: Do you think your portfolio is an assessment?

LAURIE: Yeah . . . in a way it is very much assessment because this [archive] shows how much you've improved over the years in school . . . but the IGAP testing and the California Achievement Test are things in the now. This gives you a reflection of how well you've done and how you've improved.

Laurie's presentation was award winning! With confidence and respect she told the story of her learning to our visiting teachers. Her obvious delight in getting out of her classroom endeared her to every teacher in the room. She was comfortable as she directed me in placing selected slides of her work on the overhead projector so that everyone in the audience could see her portfolio. The teachers applauded lovingly in appreciation of her well-taught lesson and Laurie beamed with pride. She couldn't wait to go home and tell her mom about this very special presentation.

Laurie taught us a lot that day. I now know that children's understanding of their portfolio is not tied to their conversation with their parents. In fact, the added task of explaining the selection of items included in the portfolio to a group of interested visitors added a new dimension of metacognitive development, beyond what emerges in conversations with those who know us well. Not being able to rely on her parents' knowledge of the specifics of context and detail forced Laurie to give concrete descriptions of those details of her learning story. She rethought her archive, and the process allowed her to make connections with prior areas of interest.

Another lesson learned is that over time, children can develop mature levels of metacognition. They can relate present work to prior interests and projects. As Laurie discovered the connection between a doll she brought to school in first grade and a research report she is writing on premature infants in fifth grade, she noted, "And now that I had an opportunity to go back and revise my stuff, I found out that I was very interested in babies and I recall that interest from first grade." This discovery has enormous implications both for the development of children's thinking skills and for the content of the portfolio as a source of curricular enrichment and extension. Portfolios are a repository for children's early ideas and interests, and can be accessed to stimulate current projects.

Listening to Laurie review her archive allowed all of us to get inside the ten-year-old mind and understand what children that age notice, what they remember, and what they consider important. Conversations with children that encourage them to make this connection between their thoughts and their learning are invaluable.

I was amazed at how expert Laurie was at remembering and retrieving the specific content of her archive. She knew the sequence and significance of each piece because she had made the decisions to include it in her portfolio. Laurie also taught us what most of us suspected, that the context of learning is far more important to the child than the content. Her fond memories of Mrs. Kappos and her clear, insightful understanding of the importance of her friendships

direct us to attend purposefully to these essential and memorable as-pects of a child's school life.

In a well-written Commentary for *Education Week*, David Tyack of Stanford University urges us to conserve what's good in education: "As I've talked with diverse people across the country, I've asked them what was their most positive experience in school. They have forgot-ten whatever fad was sweeping education or the teenage culture, but they remembered key relationships, especially with teachers. They spoke, often, with great warmth, about teachers who challenged them to use their minds to the full, who kindled enthusiasm for a subject, who honed their skills on the playing field with relentless goodwill, who were there to support them in times of stress or sadness and who knew and cared for them as individuals" (1999, p. 68).

Our conversation was an important step for Laurie, for me, and for our faculty as we continue to delve deeply into the central and fun-damental notion of children telling their own stories of learning. The confidence and ability to take a risk that Laurie demonstrated did not appear that day for the first time. It evolved gradually and required a school culture where being known matters.

Witnessing the Portfolio

What does Laurie's portfolio really tell us? How can we evaluate it? Is there some standard for a "good" portfolio? These are questions we will continue to consider as we gain more experience with port-folios and listening for children's meaning. Let me propose, how-ever, a way of structuring our inquiry.

First, we should set aside our familiar notion of evaluation as product and direct our attention to the process of portfolio. We need new language to develop our thinking so we can ask new questions. As Laurie orchestrated the sequence of slides on the overhead pro-jector, we witnessed her portfolio. To *witness* means "to see, hear, or know by personal presence or perception." When we witness a child presenting a portfolio, we become part of that presentation—we are engaged in the process with the child. As we witness we assist children to structure their thinking by engaging in substantive conversations with them along the way.

What should we look for as we witness the portfolio? The essential question is, To what extent has the child assumed ownership of the portfolio? Ownership of the portfolio is key to its potential meaning. The first grader is presented with beginning tools to help assume ownership. "What do you notice about your reading?" "Tell me the words and I'll write it on your reflection tag." "You get to choose." These are the initial encouragements to the young child that invite ownership. In these beginning stages, children rely on their teachers for support as they take small steps in gaining independence.

Over the years, children repeat this experience as they select contents for their portfolio, organize their portfolio, and record statements of value. At first, they naturally assume more traditional, teacher-based ways of collecting, selecting, and reflecting. At some point, however, children achieve a breakthrough stage where the transfer of ownership from teacher to child takes place. At that time we may observe differences in the content selected by the child, new and novel ways of organizing the portfolio, and more mature insights about specific contents, as well as about the interconnectedness of items included over time.

In witnessing the portfolio, we're looking for clarity, complexity, depth, maturity, and the connection of prior and present learning—all properties that would signal to us that the transfer of ownership has occurred. But we can't rely on our ability to see these qualities without the child's direction. In discussing Laurie's archive *with her* I could witness her portfolio in a way that I couldn't simply by examining the contents on my own. As I listened to Laurie review her work I became keenly aware of a new dimension to portfolio—the active, ongoing interaction between collector and collection that transcends the goals associated with assembling evidence of learning.

In searching for these qualities of content, organization, and evidence of metacognitive insight we should avoid preconceived notions of what we're looking for. We need to resist the temptation to grade these qualities and assign a single value to the portfolio. Why? What harm could it do? The harm is that once we set a collective, external standard the standard quickly becomes the goal, and we stop looking for the additional qualities that will, in fact, inform us about the true power of portfolios. The harm is that we stop listening for children's meaning and superimpose our own meaning.

Such a simple idea—that children could take the lead in telling the story of what and how they learn. But simple truths are not gleaned easily. Their chance discovery requires time so that they may be imagined; effort and intention so that they may be shared; patience and creativity so that they may be elaborated upon and hence, truly become a part of our learning. As the children do, we need each other's support and encouragement to pursue these possibilities. The untidy life of ideas in a school continues.

Reflection Tag

I chose this piece for my portfolio because . . .

Language is key to portfolios. New words and new ways of using words signal new thinking. Sharing the words and images that accurately portray the portfolio experience will help all involved in children's learning develop a common understanding of the unique power of portfolios.

LESSON 11

Creating a Language for Portfolios

Although portfolios are wonderful to have and exciting to develop, they do take time. It takes time to organize them and to promote their value. Teachers spend many hours in conversation with students about how to create their portfolios. Thinking through portfolio activities and getting ready for Portfolio Conferences is an extra burden for teachers' already full schedules.

Time is also needed to develop the language of portfolios, that is, words and images that differentiate portfolios from other forms of assessment. This should be language that can be clearly understood by teachers, children, and parents and that calls attention to the values associated with portfolios.

Do You Wear Shoes or a Belt?

Parents have many questions about schools, some based on issues they don't entirely understand but have heard are important. This can result in some puzzling questions as I tour prospective parents through our school.

"Is your school developmental or do you teach skills?" or "Are you a whole language school or do you teach phonics?" "Does your school use portfolios or do you give standardized tests to evaluate children?" I suspect that their concern is voiced in the first part of these questions and their hoped-for emphasis for our school is stated in the latter part. I attempt to address their concerns but I also ask them why they think these two pairings are in some way oppositional. To my mind, it's like asking if someone wears shoes or a belt.

Education is full of examples of philosophies, curricular methods, and approaches to assessment that are mistakenly characterized as conflicted. There's no inconsistency between a developmental approach and academic skills. Phonics instruction is an important component of a whole language philosophy. Portfolios and standardized tests are both used to assess children's learning. These are not opposites but rather two components of a single way of viewing instruction and assessment. So, where do these misconceptions come from?

As a society we have become accustomed to the language of debate and polarized alternatives. Deborah Tannen highlights our propensity for this disposition in her well-written book, *The Argument Culture:* "Our determination to pursue truth by setting up a fight between two sides leads us to believe that every issue has two sides—no more; no less: If both sides are given a forum to confront each other, all the relevant information will emerge, and the best case will be made for each side. But opposition does not lead to truth when an issue is not composed of two opposing sides but is a crystal of many sides. Often the truth is in the complex middle, not the oversimplified extremes" (1998, p. 10).

To find the truth in what Tannen refers to as the "complex middle," we need to pay attention to the language we use to describe these different but not opposing experiences in school. So far, it has been easier to describe what portfolios are not than to articulate a compelling vision of what portfolios are and how they work.

What Is a Portfolio?

A. A portfolio is a metaphor for a good school. It embodies the values and understanding that lead to a deeper realization of the complexities of teaching and learning. Viewing the children as competent participants in the assessment of their own learning is central to the notion of portfolio. Reflection upon self-selected samples of learning encourages the development of the metacognitive skills required for the children to understand themselves as learners.

B. A portfolio is a 9.5"x14.5" colored folder (red, yellow, blue, green) containing child-selected samples of schoolwork for the current year. The collection of grade-level folders is stored in a larger red-roped envelope that is called an archive. The child's name is affixed on a 4"x1.5" white sticker, last name first, in the upper left-hand corner of the exterior of the envelope.

One definition is abstract and carries a value. The other is concrete and easy to grasp. We need both. We began with an untidy idea—that children should and could participate in the assessment of their own learning. This abstract notion needed to be made concrete so that we could all wrap our minds around it and, most important, present the idea to our students. The colored file folders, the archive, and the Portfolio Conference Evenings all served that purpose. We dwelled on the physical aspects of portfolios for long periods and then reached back to the original concept to further our thinking. This back-and-forth dialectic between an idea and its concrete realization—between "A" and "B"—has continued to this day.

At Crow Island only a few of us remain from those first formative years of portfolios. Many new teachers have joined us. Yet our commitment to portfolios has remained unchanged. No, that's not true; our commitment has become stronger. Over these many years we've passed down the essentials of a tradition that is natural for children and energizing for teachers. We started with small steps and took the time to observe how children formally assumed ownership of a process that was theirs to begin with. We listened for children's meaning and that's how we discovered the language for portfolios. Attaching words to our ideas allowed all of us—children and teachers—to clarify meaning, affirm our learning, and thereby deepen our understanding.

We taught our students how to attach words to self-selected samples of their schoolwork. Doing so was affirmation of an achievement. The words that a child selects for a reflection tag deepen that child's understanding of self as learner. "I chose this piece for my portfolio because it shows how much I improved." Those words give meaning to that learning. Teachers listened and observed how this natural process unfolds and began to attach their own words to what they witnessed.

We don't train new teachers about how to develop portfolios. We speak portfolio at Crow Island and that's how you learn it. You hear the words and see the images that signal the values inherent in that experience. Yes, there are specific activities and rituals that serve as a structure for entering into a portfolio culture. There are videotapes to view and hundreds of archives to examine. All of this concrete evidence helps with the how-to of portfolios. And a newcomer can rely on colleagues to help out by sharing what they've learned. But most of all, these new teachers and new students experience a community of teachers committed to that untidy idea—that somehow children should have a strong, participatory role in the assessment of their own learning. New teachers experience a child's natural interest in telling the story of personal learning. They experience portfolios as embedded in a much larger and more important landscape—the values and life skills we want children to experience in their school years.

Discovering the Language of Portfolios

New language signals new thinking that in turn generates new language. The coining of words and the creation of images that are connected to those words direct us to a deeper understanding of the portfolio experience.

> "Let's go to the *Archive* to get your *portfolio*."
>
> "Remember to attach a *reflection tag* to the pieces *you choose*."
>
> "*Portfolio Evening* is a time for you to tell your parents about what you've learned."
>
> "On Portfolio Evening, you're *in charge*—you can tell *your story of how you learn*.

"That story you wrote gives *evidence* that you know how to
use capital letters and punctuation."

We have found that there is a common core of elements of the
portfolio experience regardless of a child's age:

- Child authorship
- Reflection
- Audience
- Celebration

In addition to these fundamentals, many other words and phrases
have emerged in our language over the years to help us address the
portfolio experience. We use these words and phrases with each other,
with children, or with parents to define portfolios and to communicate what portfolios can do. All these words have meanings separate
from portfolios; however, when these words are collected as a portfolio
glossary they take on a new meaning that informs us of the values and
perspective of a portfolio culture:

Achievement: Reviewing work over time and observing
   concrete evidence of skills attained and knowledge
   gained gives a child a heightened sense of achievement.
   "I like showing myself what I've done."

Archive: (1) A child's collection of work over a period of
   years that is contained in a 10"x15" red-roped envelope.
   An archive contains all of the individual yearly
   portfolios. (2) The place where the individual child
   archives are kept in the school. At Crow Island we
   designated shelves in our Library/Resource Center for our
   School Archive, which also includes school photographs,
   articles, and books written about our school.

Ask Me About: An organizing outline to assist children with the Portfolio Conference with their parents. Similar to a table of contents, an *Ask Me About* cover sheet lists particular features of the portfolio that the child wants to remember to show or comment on.

Audience: A specified audience for a portfolio presentation. At Crow Island we designated parents as the primary audience. Other audience possibilities could be siblings, older or younger students in the school, teachers in the school, peer-level classroom of students, senior citizens in the community.

Celebration: An essential component of the portfolio process. A group celebration of learning. The Portfolio Conference Evening is one expression of that celebration.

Choice, Choose: Making choices about the contents of the portfolio, critical to the child's involvement in the process. Depending on the age of the student, this process is facilitated by conversation with teachers, older students, or peers.

Content: The specific selections of work contained in the portfolio. (See related discussion of content, ownership, and purpose of the portfolio in Lesson 4.)

Conversation: Children in conversation with their teachers, older students, and peers, making decisions about the content of the portfolio. Children talking to children about common experiences and lessons learned; proven to be a very powerful resource for our students as they consider how best to tell their individual story of learning. Children in conversation with their parents about the content of their portfolio reinforces the notions of achievement, competence and involvement in learning.

Curriculum Overview: A single-page grade-level overview of curriculum, composed of mini-statements of curricular content, objectives, and materials for each reporting period of the school year for all subject areas. This overview is reprinted on the reverse side of the Learning Experience Form.

Evidence of learning: In reflecting upon selected pieces of schoolwork, children discover evidence of particular skills or achievements. For example, a story written in second grade may be evidence of when the child learned to begin a sentence with a capital letter.

Favorites: Children may organize a portfolio by selecting their *favorite* pieces of work. Other ways to organize a portfolio are chronologically or by subject area.

Freedom: Children experience freedom of expression as they make decisions about how best to tell their unique story of learning. The format allows for diversity and individual interpretations.

Generative: Portfolios inspire children and teachers to think about learning in new ways. Reflective conversations with teacher, peers, and parents generate further purposes for the portfolio.

Goals: Children articulate learning and behavioral goals as they review their current levels of performance in the portfolio review.

History: Children examine the history of their learning through the portfolio process. This concept is presented at different grade levels through allusions to baby books and timelines of our lives.

Internalized: A child's unique story of learning, internalized because that child is the author of that story. Only the creator of the portfolio truly understands all the interconnections among the various pieces of learning selected.

Learning buddy: Buddy relationships provide opportunities for classrooms of older and younger children to form alliances around learning activities.

Learning experiences: Instances of children's learning. It is a more global term that includes all subject areas and acknowledges that children's learning takes place outside the school setting as well as within the many classrooms, studios, and gymnasiums of the school setting. To communicate this message to parents we revised our progress-reporting form and called it the Learning Experiences Form.

Menu: A commonly used way of organizing a table of contents for a portfolio. Children prepare a cover sheet for their portfolio and archive titled "Ask Me About." It assists children in remembering what aspects of their portfolio and archive they want to highlight in conference with their parents.

Metacognition, Metacognitive: The child's conscious knowledge of personal abilities, skills, and interests; that is, "knowing what we know."

Multiple intelligences: Howard Gardner's theory of multiple intelligences asserts that there are at least seven different kinds of intelligences: Musical, Linguistic, Logical/Mathematical, Spatial, Bodily-Kinesthetic, Interpersonal, and Intrapersonal. (In later work, Gardner notes possible additional intelligences, that is, Naturalist and Spiritual or Existential—see *Intelligence Reframed,* 1999, p. 66.)

Organize: Children can organize their portfolios chronologically, according to subjects, or by favorites.

Purpose: Our purpose for the portfolio is to engage the child in evaluating personal learning. In collecting and reflecting upon self-selected work, children learn how to tell their unique story of learning. (See related discussion of content, ownership, and purpose of the portfolio in Lesson 4.)

Ownership: Ownership of the portfolio is determined by its purpose and by who selects its content—teacher, child, or both in collaboration. (See related discussion of content, ownership, and purpose of the portfolio in Lesson 4.)

Notice: As in, "What do you notice?" A phrase that prompts the child into reflective thinking. In comparing a piece of writing from the beginning of the year with a current story children may notice that their printing is smaller and that they now use space between the words.

Passion: Recurrent themes or projects are referred to as a child's passion.

Portfolio: A 9.5"x14.5" colored folder (red, first; yellow, second; blue, third; green, fourth) containing child-selected samples of schoolwork for the current year. The collection of grade level folders is stored in a larger red-roped envelope that is called an archive. The child's name is affixed on a 4"x1.5" white sticker, last name first, in the upper left-hand corner of the exterior of the envelope. The word also applies to the black binders used for the same purpose in the fifth grade.

Portfolio Conference Evening: One evening of the school year when children are given the genuine responsibility of presenting their portfolio to their parents. At this conference, students are expected to explain the process by which the materials in the portfolio have been selected, the self-reflection it involved, the conversations with the teacher that spurred particular directions to be taken, and any other aspects of their "learning story" they wish to share. The parent-child conference is approximately thirty to forty-five minutes in length.

Reflection: Thinking about your learning—remembering what is important to you. Comparing pieces of your writing or math work, for example, from early in the year with work you are doing now—what do you notice?

Reflection Tag: A brief written statement prepared by the child (or dictated to the teacher or a learning buddy) that indicates a rationale for including a piece of work in the portfolio. These reflections are written on small tags of paper with the introductory phrase, "I chose this piece for my portfolio because. . . ."

Story: Through the portfolio process a child is able to tell a unique story of learning.

Unique: Each child's story of learning; unique to that student.

Video: In addition to children's individual stories of learning, each classroom experiences a collective learning story that is important to relate. The production of a classroom videotape is yet another dimension of portfolio development, the classroom portfolio. This video is intended to portray a day in the life of this particular group of students, including the learning that takes place in special subject areas of Art, Music, Physical Education, Spanish, and Library and Technology. In addition, many classroom videotapes include recess activities and selected field trips. The classroom video of approximately twenty minutes in length is an important collaborative segment of the Portfolio Conference celebration.

These are some of the words that have helped us in thinking about portfolio. Most reflect our concentration on the child's needs and strengths. In that way we have discovered what can be termed the *essence of portfolio*—its internal rationale. When you encounter the essence of a subject, it's readily apparent to all concerned. Once an essential meaning is discovered, the language, imagination, and energy flow freely. A release of truths that the whole group shares is the core of the fundamental experience.

CONCLUSION

Lessons Learned About Portfolios

We have discovered that the benefits of portfolios go far beyond their usefulness as a tool to judge the child's work. Portfolios allow students to explore their learning and provide a rich array of interactions designed to motivate students of all abilities. Compiling a portfolio has direct and observable impact on the development of children's metacognitive strategies. In addition, portfolios can be an integral tool for effective staff development in that they provide a means for teachers to reflect deeply about their teaching methods and curriculum. Portfolios support a reflective school culture for children and teachers alike.

An important lesson gleaned from our work is that the ownership of the portfolio will dictate its purpose and contents. Deciding whether the teacher, the child, or both teacher and child own the portfolio has much to do with how it will evolve. We recognize that the decision of what portfolios should include may be made by administrators or committees. But teachers have always managed to cope with such directives and make them productive in the classroom. Teachers may decide for themselves that they wish to direct the portfolio process more closely and focus on a single subject area. The point is that we need to recognize that there are many different ways of thinking about portfolios. We need to be clear about the ownership so that teachers and students can proceed to organize portfolios in accordance with that understanding.

For the child, the impact of portfolio upon metacognitive development may be the most significant of its benefits. Gathering and thinking about work contributes significantly to a child's self-understanding. This is vital to accomplishing internal goals that go far beyond what the child needs to know for tomorrow's math lesson or to do well on a standardized test. Having a measure to assess personal strengths and weaknesses lets the child move toward achieving an internal standard of accountability. Beyond a child's school experiences, the self-knowledge gleaned through self-assessment is an invaluable tool for lifelong learning. Portfolio development provides remarkable opportunities for preparing to present oneself in the world with confidence and insight.

Portfolios let the child learn from the assessment process while it is occurring. Even the youngest students have the ability to collect, organize, and reflect upon a collection of their schoolwork and the process of their learning. Over time, and with direct support and guidance from their teachers, children are able to comprehend and assess the trends of their understandings and to make meaningful connections between prior and present learning experiences. In addition, these young students are able to articulate appropriate goals relevant to future learning.

For teachers and parents, the notion of *learning from the assessment* in addition to *assessing what has been learned* is a dramatic departure from ingrained assumptions about how to judge schoolwork. Portfolios require an entirely different way of thinking about the teacher-student interaction. Sharing the evaluative role with a child, allowing the choice of content to be the child's work, and developing the metacognitive questions that will assist the children in determining their own strategies toward stated goals are all very new concepts.

I have been asked whether our school's scores on standardized tests have risen since we began our work with portfolios. The assumption is that when students take ownership of learning and engage in metacognitive reflection, we should see gains in other achievement measures. The answer is yes and no. Yes, our scores on standardized tests have risen. And no, I can't make the case for a direct causal link between our work with portfolios and gains in standardized test scores at this time. There are many other variables that can account for the test score gains—changes in curriculum and staff and revisions of testing instruments over that period of time. Also the ownership in learning that children experience in compiling their portfolios is very different from their experience of taking a standardized test. As noted in Chapter Ten, I asked Laurie about the differences in these experiences.

PRINCIPAL: Do you think your portfolio is an assessment?

LAURIE: Yeah . . . in a way it is very much assessment because this [archive] shows how much you've improved over the years in school . . . but the IGAP testing and the California Achievement Test are things in the now. This gives you a reflection of how well you've done and how you've improved.

The portfolio experience and its influence and consequences on standardized test scores is certainly an area for further rich study.

Schools seldom maintain the long-term focus and energy on a program or idea that allows us to separate the very best in education from what is standard or ordinary. This book is a collection of lessons learned over a period of many years by the students, teachers, and principal of one school, about one idea—that children can gain insights into the process of their learning through portfolios. Spending so many years exploring this hypothesis has allowed us to discover subtleties that can only be uncovered by sustained focus and an enormous amount of experience.

Our long-term experience has given us a chance to rethink our view of the teaching-learning interaction and the process of assessment. The possibilities that portfolios provide should persuade all of us to move forward in affirming the premise that children can become competent participants in the assessment of their own learning. The first bold step is allowing the children to take the lead.

APPENDIX

Philosophy of the Winnetka Public Schools

Background

The Winnetka Public Schools have a long tradition of leadership in public education. Under the guidance of community leaders and prominent educators such as Carleton Washburne, Francis Parker, and Frederick Burk the schools sought "to stimulate and help each child to develop his own personal and social potentialities in accordance with his individual design of growth" (Washburne and Marland, 1963 p. 22]). The distinguishing characteristics of education in Winnetka which came to prominence in the 1920s remain vital and effective today. Some of these characteristics are subtle and abstract, dealing with the spirit and commitment of the faculty and community; others are more concrete. The specific goals of the Winnetka Schools outlined in this paper grow from the philosophy of individualized education and from the continued involvement of teachers and community in the educational process.

Carleton Washburne wrote in 1940 in *A Living Philosophy of Education* that "a philosophy of education, evolved by those who are living among children, helping them, and being taught and guided by them, is itself living, and like all living things, it is ever-changing" [p. xv]. Twenty years later, Sidney Marland wrote, "as the faculty and administration change, it is important that all concerned, periodically, have a hand in establishing new goals and procedures. Otherwise, something less than whole-hearted commitment is likely to follow" [Washburne and Marland, 1963, p. 195].

At present we are once again engaged in evaluating our goals and defining the objectives of education in Winnetka. Teachers and administrators are involved in examining current research on children's learning, and evaluating their own observations and experience. These processes, together with our beliefs and educational objectives which are outlined below, guide curriculum development.

Beliefs

We believe that our schools have served and should continue to serve as an education laboratory for the pursuit and discovery of ever better ways to teach and to learn. We place high emphasis on providing a learning environment which will encourage the child's maximum capabilities. Fulfillment of the individual must take into account the wide spectrum of differences in readiness and in ability. We also believe that our schools have a responsibility to prepare children for active and constructive roles in the larger society.

In summary, we believe that our primary concerns are (1) commitment to the individual, (2) emphasis on intellectual excellence, and (3) preservation of the ideals of social responsibility and equal opportunity in the school setting and in the larger society.

Educational Objectives

Within the context of the beliefs stated above, and the historical evolution of our community and our schools, we seek for all Winnetka children a learning environment which will foster the following broad objectives, which in turn are implemented by the more specific curricula of the schools.

1. Give primary concern to intellectual growth.

Though the school shares with other institutions the responsibility for social, emotional, spiritual, and physical growth, the primary responsibility of the school is the intellectual growth of the child. Intellectual growth means much more than an increasing competence in the academic content of the curriculum. We must also stimulate in the child a love of learning and a questioning mind. We teach children that learning is its own reward and that asking the right questions is as important as finding the answers. Learning can best flourish when teachers, supported by adequate materials and sound academic preparation, create a climate in which children are genuinely desirous of learning.

Some ways of achieving this climate are social studies units such as ancient civilizations which offer a wide scope of learning activities. Typically such units include reading of history and biography, participation in dramatic play, craft projects, and small group work, and tie-ins with music and art.

2. Teach the basic skills thoroughly.

We seek for each child a mastery of the tools of learning which are essential to the more abstract learning and thinking which follows. To read well, and with appropriate pace and comprehension, to express oneself effectively in speech and writing, to perform with precision the fundamental mathematical processes, and to have a command of the scientific process of thought are reasonable expectations for nearly every child by the end of eighth grade. The pace of learning the basic skills is determined by the child's level of intellectual development and by his readiness; children differ far more widely than most people realize in their readiness and ability to learn school subjects. The curriculum must provide the step-by-step content requirements consistent with the mental age and maturity of the child and must be sufficiently flexible to challenge the fast learner and be within the grasp of the slow learner.

The goal card is the instrument used in the Winnetka Public Schools in first through fifth grade to outline the progression through which basic skills are developed. Since each child has his own goal card, adaptations are made to accommodate each student's learning style, with deletions and additions made according to the child's individual needs.

Example: The curriculum in mathematics includes student textbooks developed by the faculty which provide sequential learnings and self-checking answers. The students do not proceed to higher expectations until they fully understand the prerequisite material.

3. Consider the child a total human being.

A balanced educational program takes into account the realities of physical, emotional, and social growth as well as intellectual development. The classroom and the school offer many opportunities for growth when guided by sensitive and caring adults. It is our practice for all faculty to work together, employing their combined expertise in understanding and guiding each child's development. The Department of Pupil Services helps parents and teachers in this process. This department has the services of psychologists, social workers, teachers of learning disabilities, speech therapists and nurses.

Example: School-home communication helps fulfill this objective. Parent-teacher conferences provide the opportunity to exchange information and advice concerning the child's social and emotional growth. The Department of Pupil Services is available to any parents and teachers seeking help and advice in the area of child guidance.

4. Discover and respond to the variety of interest and talents of all children.

The schools are heavily committed to the reality of individual differences. Using all available resources, teachers constantly seek ways to help students realize their full potential. Children of all abilities and needs can find fulfillment not only in academic learning, but also in art, music, drama, journalism, woodworking, home arts, creative writing, and in leadership roles and participation in group projects, such as service projects and social events. Helping children discover their special interests and abilities will assist them in later life to choose the kind of work they can do best and that will be the most satisfying. Developing children's interests and talents will also increase their range of choice for enjoyable, productive uses of their leisure time, an increasingly important goal.

Example: Throughout the district talent pool volunteers work with individual students in areas of their special interest and needs. At the junior high, classes in leadership and creativity are offered to those students who demonstrate potential in these areas.

5. Foster physical and mental health.

The attitudes and skills relating to physical education, physiology, including sex education, and health and safety education are part of the child's total growth. Vigorous physical activity appropriate to the maturity of the child develops strong, healthy bodies. The playing field and the gym offer many opportunities for learning cooperation, fair play, and leadership.

Mental health implies a personal sense of well-being and leads to effective learning. Teachers foster good mental health by accepting the child, by creating an atmosphere of clearly defined limits and expectations, and by ensuring frequent realistic experiences of success at the child's own level.

Example: Our design for instruction places the students largely in competition with themselves. Teachers individualize the meaning of "success" knowing that each child must frequently feel successful. What is success for one child may be a very low order of work for another.

Our reporting procedures, which are ungraded and anecdotal in the lower grades, ease gradually to more traditional grading in the junior high. In this way children can gain a sense of satisfaction from their own performance rather than experience failure when measuring themselves against a personally unobtainable standard.

6. Prepare the child for informed and responsible citizenship.

This requires thinking in terms of the well-being of the community, the nation and all mankind, rather than in purely personal terms. Such thinking has to be developed through social experiences— through cooperative work and play, and through seeing the connection between oneself and one's neighbor.

Example: Through the organized and supervised playground program the children learn the value of team work, and such traits as good sportsmanship and endurance. Through student committees, student councils and other forms of student responsibility, they learn to practice citizenship as a matter of daily living together in the school community. Through group activities and service projects such as a class mural, producing a video-tape, food collections, they learn to contribute their individual talents to a common goal. Through dramatization, where the children plan their own plays and make their own costumes and scenery, they learn to work together, to feel the dependence of the group on each individual doing his own part well.

7. Provide a setting which stimulates aesthetic development.

Through rich experiences and exposures, children can internalize an appreciation for beauty. Art, music, literature, drama, speech, creative writing and craft work are the more obvious channels for the cultivation of aesthetic values. Building awareness of scientific phenomena and mathematical patterns also contribute to a child's aesthetic development.

Example: The arts are widely supported in the schools through the elective program, through assemblies bringing accomplished artists and musicians into the schools, and through those field trips which expose students to different kinds of artistic expression.

8. Encourage the pursuit of excellence.

With knowledge of each student, teachers establish criteria for excellence, and accept only the best that each can produce. Satisfaction and success follow when both teacher and student have extended themselves to the fullest.

Example: Students are encouraged to work on special projects either individually or in groups and to value the work of others as well as their own. High expectations and standards are set for the project. Children are helped to see all projects through to completion, and are given recognition for effort and for quality of work.

January 23, 1981

THE AUTHOR

Elizabeth A. Hebert has been principal of Crow Island School in Winnetka, Illinois, since 1984. She earned both her B.S. degree in education of the hearing-impaired with a minor in classical studies (1972) and her M.A. degree (1973) in communicative disorders from Northwestern University's School of Speech. She earned her Ph.D. in educational administration (1983) from Loyola University of Chicago.

Hebert has taught hearing-impaired children in the Chicago Public Schools and held supervisory and administrative positions in special education in the Chicago suburban area. She has lectured and written extensively on the topics of student portfolios, school architecture, inclusion of special needs children in the classroom, and school leadership.

BIBLIOGRAPHY

Archbald, D., and Newmann, F. *Beyond Standardized Testing: Assessing Authentic Academic Achievement in the Secondary School*. Reston, Va.: National Association of Secondary School Principals, 1988.

Ball, D. L. "What Do Students Know? Facing Challenges of Distance, Context, and Desire in Trying to Hear Children." In B. J. Biddle, T. L. Good, and I. F. Goodson (eds.), *International Handbook of Teachers and Teaching*, Vol. 1. Dordrecht, The Netherlands: Kluwer, 1997, pp. 769–818.

Bereiter, C., and Scardamalia, M. "Child as Co-investigator: Helping Children Gain Insight into Their Own Mental Processes." In S. Paris, G. Olson, and H. Stevenson (eds.), *Learning and Motivation in the Classroom*. Hillsdale, N.J.: Erlbaum, 1983. pp. 61–82.

Bird, L. "Getting Started with Portfolios." In K. Goodman, L. B. Bird, and Y. Goodman, *The Whole Language Catalog Supplement on Authentic Assessment*, 1992, pp. 122–129.

Carini, P. F. "Valuing the Immeasurable." In *Starting Strong: A Different Look at Children's Schools and Standards*. New York: Teachers College Press, in press, chapter 2.

Cole, K., and others. "Portfolio Assessment: Challenges in Secondary Education." *High School Journal*, Apr.-May 1997, 80, 261–272. Chapel Hill: School of Education, University of North Carolina.

Crow Island School, Winnetka, Ill. *Annual Report 2000–01*.

Eisner, E. *Cognition and Curriculum Reconsidered*. New York: Teachers College Press, 1994.

Eisner, E. "What Does It Mean to Say a School Is Doing Well?" *Phi Delta Kappan*, 2001, 82(5), 367–372.

Fry, P. S., and Lupart, J. L. *Cognitive Processes in Children's Learning*. Springfield, Ill.: Thomas, 1987.

Gardner, H. *Frames of Mind: The Theory of Multiple Intelligences*. New York: Basic Books, 1983.

Gardner, H. *Intelligence Reframed*. New York: Basic Books 1999.

Gilbert, J. *Portfolio Resource Guide: Creating and Using Portfolios in the Classroom*. Ottowa, Ks.: Writing Conference, 1993.

Gipps, C. V. "Socio-cultural Aspects of Assessment." In P. D. Pearson and A. Iran-Nejad (eds.), *Review of Research in Education* (Vol. 4). Washington, D.C.: American Educational Research Association, 1999, pp. 335–392.

Gong, B., and Reidy, E. "Assessment and Accountability in Kentucky's School Reform." In J. Baron and D. Palmer Wolf (eds.), *Performance-Based Assessment: Challenges and Possibilities. Ninety-Fifth Yearbook of the National Society for the Study of Education, Part I*. Chicago: University of Chicago Press, 1996, pp. 215–233.

Gordon, E., and Bonilla-Bowman, C. "Can Performance Based Assessments Contribute to the Achievement of Educational Equity?" In J. Baron and D. Palmer Wolf (eds.), *Performance-Based Assessment: Challenges and Possibilities. Ninety-Fifth Yearbook of the National Society for the Study of Education, Part I*. Chicago: University of Chicago Press, 1996, pp. 32–51.

Grace, C., and Shores, E. *The Portfolio and Its Use: Developmentally Appropriate Assessment of Young Children*. Little Rock, Ark.: Southern Association on Children Under Six, 1992.

Graue, M. E. "Integrating Theory and Practice Through Instructional Assessment." *Educational Assessment*, 1983, *1*(4), 283–309.

Graves, D. H., and Sunstein, B. (eds.), *Portfolio Portraits*. Portsmouth, N.H.: Heinemann, 1992.

Gullo, D. *Understanding Assessment and Evaluation in Early Childhood Education*. New York: Teachers College Press, 1994.

Hansen, J. *When Learners Evaluate*. Portsmouth, N.H.: Heinemann, 1998.

Haroutunian-Gordon, S. *Turning the Soul: Teaching Through Conversation in the High School*. Chicago: University of Chicago Press, 1991.

Hebert, E. A. "Portfolios Invite Reflection—From Students and Staff." *Educational Leadership*, 1992, 49(8), 58–61.

Hebert, E. A. "Portfolio Assessment: Children Talk About Their Own Learning," *Winnetka Alliance for Early Childhood Newsletter*, 1995, 6(1), 1.

Hebert, E. A. "An Inclusive Approach to Assessing Children's Learning: Conversations About Portfolios." In E. Hebert (ed.), *Schools for Everyone: A New Perspective on Inclusion*. New Directions for School Leadership, no. 3. San Francisco: Jossey-Bass, 1997, pp. 39–50.

Hebert, E. A. "Design Matters: How School Environment Affects Children." *Educational Leadership*, 1998, 56(1), 69–70.

Hebert, E. A. "Lessons Learned About Student Portfolios." *Phi Delta Kappan*, 1998, 79(8), 583–585.

Hebert, E., with Schultz, L. "The Power of Portfolios." *Educational Leadership*, 1996, 53(7), 70–71.

Hill, B. C., and Ruptic, C. *Practical Aspects of Authentic Assessment: Putting the Pieces Together*. Norwood, Mass.: Christopher-Gordon, 1994.

Hinchcliffe, V., and Roberts, M. "Developing Social Cognition and Metacognition." In B. Smith (ed.), *Interactive Approaches to the Education of Children with Severe Learning Difficulties*. Birmingham, England: Westhill College, 1987, p. 81.

Jervis, K. *Eyes on the Child: Three Portfolio Stories*. New York: Teachers College Press, 1996.

Jervis, K., and Montag, C. (eds.). *Progressive Education for the 1990s: Transforming Practice*. New York: Teachers College Press, 1991.

Johnson, D., and Silverman, S. "Seeing the Child Through Portfolio Collection." In A. Costa and B. Kallick, *Assessment in the Learning Organization: Shifting the Paradigm*. Alexandria, Va.: Association for Supervision and Curriculum Development, 1995, pp. 195–204.

Koretz, D., and others. "Can Portfolios Assess Student Performance and Influence Instruction? The 1991–92 Vermont Experience." Los Angeles: National Center for Research on Evaluation, Standards, and Student Testing, Dec. 1993.

Koretz, D., and others. "The Vermont Portfolio Assessment Program: Findings and Implications." *Educational Measurement: Issues and Practice*, 1994, 13(3), 5–16.

LeMahieu, P., Gitomer, D., and Eresh, J. "Portfolios in Large-Scale Assessment: Difficult But Not Impossible." *Educational Measurement: Issues and Practice*, 1995, 14(3), 11–28.

Lemann, N. *The Big Test: The Secret History of the American Meritocracy.* New York: Farrar, Straus & Giroux, 1999.

Levine, M. *All Kinds of Minds: A Young Student's Book About Learning Abilities and Learning Disorders.* Cambridge, Mass.: Educator's Publishing Services, 1993.

Madaus, G., and others. *Testing and Evaluation: Learning from the Projects We Fund.* New York: Council for Aid to Education, 1992.

Martin-Kniep, G. O. *Why Am I Doing This? Purposeful Teaching Through Portfolio Assessment.* Portsmouth, N.H.: Heinemann, 1998.

Marzano, R. *Transforming Classroom Grading.* Alexandria, Va.: Association for Supervision and Curriculum Development, 2000.

McCombs, B. "Issues in the Measurement of Standardized Tests of Primary Motivational Variables Related to Self-Regulated Learning." Paper presented at the annual meeting of the American Educational Research Association, Washington, D.C., April, 1987.

Mills, R. "Statewide Portfolio Assessment: The Vermont Experience." In J. Baron and D. Palmer Wolf (eds.), *Performance-Based Assessment: Challenges and Possibilities. Ninety-Fifth Yearbook of the National Society for the Study of Education, Part I.* Chicago: University of Chicago Press, 1996, pp. 192–214.

Montgomery, B. "Portfolios as Critical Anchors for Continuous Learning." In A. Costa and B. Kallick, *Assessment in the Learning Organization: Shifting the Paradigm.* Alexandria, Va.: Association for Supervision and Curriculum Development, 1995, pp. 205–210.

Murphy, S., and Smith, M. A. *Writing Portfolios: A Bridge from Teaching to Assessment.* Ontario, Canada: Pippin Publishing, 1992.

Newmann, F. "Linking Restructuring to Authentic Student Achievement." *Phi Delta Kappan,* 1991, 73(6), 458–463.

Paley, V. "On Listening to What the Children Say." *Harvard Educational Review,* 1986, 56(2), 122–131.

Paulsen, P. R., and Paulsen, F. L. "Portfolios: Stories of Knowing." In P. H. Dreyer (ed.), *Claremont Reading Conference 55th Yearbook—Knowing: The Power of Stories.* Claremont, Calif.: Claremont Reading Conference Center for the Developmental Studies, Claremont Graduate School, 1991, pp. 294–303.

Perrone, V. (ed.). *Expanding Student Assessment.* Alexandria, Va.: Association for Supervision and Curriculum Development, 1991.

Putnam, R. T., and Borko, H. "Teacher Learning: Implications of New Views of Cognition." In B. J. Biddle, T. L. Good, and I. F. Goodson (eds.), *International Handbook of Teachers and Teaching*, Vol. 2. Dordrecht, The Netherlands: Kluwer, 1997, pp. 1223–1296.

Resnick, L. *Education and Learning to Think*. Washington, D.C.: National Academy Press, 1987.

Sacks, P. *Standardized Minds: The High Price of America's Testing Culture and What We Can Do to Change It*. Cambridge, Mass.: Perseus Books, 1999.

Sergiovanni, T. *Leadership for the Schoolhouse: How Is It Different—Why Is It Important?* San Francisco: Jossey-Bass, 1996.

Sergiovanni, T. *The Lifeworld of Leadership: Creating Culture, Community, and Personal Meaning in Our Schools*. San Francisco: Jossey-Bass, 1999.

Shephard, L. "The Role of Assessment in a Learning Culture." *Educational Researcher*, 2000, 29(7), 4–14.

Sizer, T. *Horace's School: Redesigning the American High School*. Boston: Houghton Mifflin, 1992.

Spaulding, C. "The Motivation to Read and Write." In J. W. Irwin and N. A. Doyle (eds.), *Reading/Writing Connections: Learning from Research*. Newark, Del.: International Reading Association, 1991, pp. 177–201.

Stevenson, C. "Evaluation and Assessment: Understanding What's Happening." In C. Stevenson, *Teaching Ten to Fourteen Year Olds*. New York: Longman, 1992, pp. 242–272.

Tannen, D. *The Argument Culture: Moving from Debate to Dialogue*. New York: Random House, 1998, p. 10.

Tyack, D. "Needed: More Educational Conservationists?" *Education Week Commentary*, 1999, 18(41), 68.

Washburne, C. *A Living Philosophy of Education*. New York: John Day, 1940.

Washburne, C., and Marland, S. *Winnetka: The History and Significance of an Educational Experiment*. Upper Saddle River, N.J.: Prentice Hall, 1963.

Wiggins, G. *Assessing Student Performance*. San Francisco: Jossey-Bass, 1993.

Wiggins, G. "Creating Tests Worth Taking." *Educational Leadership*, 1992, 49(8), 26–33.

Wolf, D., Bixby, J., Glenn, J., and Gardner, H. "To Use Their Minds Well: Investigating New Forms of Student Assessment." In G. Grant (ed.),

Review of Research in Education 17, Washington, D.C.: American Educational Research Association, 1991, pp. 31–74.

Wolf, D., and Reardon, S. "Access to Excellence Through New Forms of Student Assessment." In J. Baron and D. Palmer Wolf (eds.), *Performance-Based Assessment: Challenges and Possibilities. Ninety-Fifth Yearbook of the National Society for the Study of Education, Part I*. Chicago: University of Chicago Press, 1996, pp. 1–31.

Worthen, B. R. "Critical Issues That Will Determine the Future of Alternative Assessment." *Phi Delta Kappan*, Feb. 1993, pp. 444–454.

Yancey, K. B. *Portfolios in the Writing Classroom*. Urbana, Ill.: National Council of Teachers of English, 1992.

Index

A

Accommodation of exclusion, 64, 67
Achievement portfolio, 45
Annual Report (Crow Island School), 105
Archive. *See* Portfolio archive
The Argument Culture (Tannen), 122
Art: classroom video portfolio on, 94,
    130; Curriculum Overview on, 35.
    See also Non-core curriculum
Ask Me About cover sheet, 126, 128
Assessment: fitting portfolios into school
    program of, 104–109; notion of learn-
    ing from, 132; of own learning by
    children, 55–56; standardized tests
    used in, 67–68

B

Benchmarks. *See* Learning benchmarks
Bereiter, C., 51, 54
Bird, L., 43
Bodily-Kinesthetic intelligence, 13, 128
Bonilla-Brown, C., 52
Bulletin (Crow Island School): Faculty
    Portfolio Panel notice in, 101; stan-
    dardized testing meeting notice in, 104

C

Carini, P., 2
CAT (California Achievement Test),
    104, 105, 108, 115

Chicago Public Schools, 112
Child portfolio ownership: affirming,
    112–117; defining teacher vs., 43–44;
    internalized learning through, 127;
    witnessing the, 117–119
Child Reflection, 33, 36
Child-centered philosophy: portfolio-
    child connection and, 7; Winnetka
    Public Schools, 135–141
Child-organized portfolio, 46
Children. *See* Students
Children's abilities: acknowledging/af-
    firming spectrum of, 11–13; competi-
    tive sorting according to, 67–68;
    multiple intelligences model on,
    13–15
Classroom environment, 74, 75–78
Classroom video portfolio, 94–96, 130
Co-investigators/coinvestigation, 54
Collaborative learning environment,
    53–56
Communication. *See* Conversations;
    Language
"Complex middle" truth, 122
Conversations: high school student
    teaching using, 55; parent-teacher
    planning, 100–104; portfolio lan-
    guage used in, 126; reflective, 53–56;
    substantive, 54. *See also* Language
Core curriculum: Learning Experiences
    Form applied to, 27; Winnetka Public
    Schools emphasis on basic skills,
    137–138

Crow Island School: assessment program used by, 104–109; building goals for, 107–109; communication between student home and, 106–107; continued commitment to portfolios by, 123–124; portfolio archive created for, 78–83; reporting form changes by, 24–36; specific design features of, 76–78. *See also* Winnetka Public Schools

Curriculum: acknowledging importance of non-core, 27–28; Gardner's theory applied to, 16; lack of formal reporting on non-core, 24; Learning Experiences Form report on, 30–33, 34–35; portfolio contents on, 42–43; portfolios as, 52; school organization of, 15–16

Curriculum Overview: designing, 31, 33; as part of student assessment, 106; portfolio language to discuss, 126–127; sample of completed, 34–35

Curriculum portfolio, 45

D

Department of Public Services (Winnetka Public Schools), 138

E

Easy/hard questionnaire, 4–5, 6

Education: language of, 122; Winnetka Public Schools philosophy of, 135–141

Education Week, 117

Environment. *See* Learning environments

Essence of portfolio, 130

Existential intelligence, 13, 128

F

Faculty Portfolio Panel, 101

Favorite pieces of work, 127

Fifth graders: Conference preparation for parents of, 104; portfolio experience of, 72–73

First graders: Conference preparation for parents of, 103; by portfolio experience, 69–70; visit to kindergartner students by, 3

"Floating circles," 24–25

Fourth grade portfolio experience, 72

Fourth graders, Conference preparation for parents of, 103–104

Freedom of expression, 127

Fry, P. S., 51

G

Gardner, H., 13, 128

Gardner's Multiple Intelligences Theory: applied to children's learning, 13–14; applied to curriculum, 16; connecting teacher experiences to, 17–20; as passageway to portfolios, 10

Goals, 127

Gordon, E., 52

H

Haroutunian-Gordon, S., 55

Hebert, E. A., 143

Hinchcliffe, V., 51

History of learning: portfolio process as, 127; reflection tags as, 60–61

Home-school communication, 106–107. *See also* Conversations

Horace's School (Sizer), 53

I

IEP (Individualized Education Plan), 64

IEP Annual reviews, 108

IGAP (Illinois Goals Assessment Program), 108, 115

Inclusion need, 63–65

Independent learning projects, 65–66

Individual learning needs: exploring prior topics of interest as, 66; facilitating inclusion, 63–65; independent learning projects filling, 65–66; learning differences and, 67–68; reflection tags supporting, 62; Winnetka Public Schools focus on, 138–139. *See also* Students

Inside language, 29–30

Intelligence Reframed (Gardner), 13

Interpersonal intelligence, 13, 128

Intrapersonal intelligence, 13, 128

ISAT (Illinois Standards Achievement Tests), 104, 105

J

Jeff's story, 17–20

K

Kindergartner students: Conference preparation for parents of, 102; portfolio experience of, 68–69; visits by first graders to, 2

L

Language: creating portfolio, 121–130; of education, 122; as key to portfolios, 120; second grade children's level of, 71; of self-reflection, 51, 53–56, 72; teacher inside vs. outside, 29–30; for witnessing the portfolio, 117–118. *See also* Conversations
Language Arts Curriculum Overview, 34. *See also* Core curriculum
Laurie's portfolio presentation, 113–117, 118, 133
Learning: application of multiple intelligences model to, 13–15; child's assessment of own, 55–56; collaborative environment promoting, 53–56; confidence from metacognitive associations with, 52; designing new form of reporting on, 24–26; environments of, 15–16; from assessment, 132; how children think of, 10; internalized through portfolio, 127; metacognition component of, 51; portfolio language to examine, 127; portfolios for thinking about, 52; school/classroom environment and, 74
Learning benchmarks: child recognition of, 3; easy/hard questionnaire facilitating, 4–5, 6; of kindergarten students, 68–69
"Learning buddies" relationships, 69, 88, 127
Learning environments: created in school or classroom, 74; message of, 75–78; reflective conversation to create, 53–56; various types of, 15–16
Learning experiences: Crow Island School adoption of, 25–26; portfolio language definition of, 128
Learning Experiences Form: Child Reflection added to, 33, 36; Curriculum Overview added to, 31, 33, 34–35; example of blank, 28; labeling tabs of, 27, 29; reporting children's growth using, 30–33; sample of completed, 32

Library/Resource Center: classroom portfolio video on, 94, 130; Crow Island School portfolio archive in, 79–80, 88; Curriculum Overview on, 35. *See also* Non-core curriculum
Linguistic intelligence, 13, 128
A Living Philosophy of Education (Washburne), 135
Logical-Mathematical intelligence, 13, 128
Lupart, J. L., 51

M

Marland, S., 135, 136
Math: Curriculum Overview on, 34; Winnetka Public Schools curriculum in, 138. *See also* Core curriculum
McCombs, B., 51
Menu, 128
Mesic, P., 82
Metacognition: attaching meaning to work and, 70; children's development of mature, 116; defining, 51, 128; portfolio impact on development of, 132; portfolios as curricular framework for, 52; reflection tags as history of, 60–61; reflective conversation promoting, 53–56. *See also* Learning
Multiple intelligences: defining, 128; staff development of their own, 26–27
Multiple Intelligences Theory. *See* Gardner's Multiple Intelligences Theory
Music: classroom portfolio video on, 94, 130; Curriculum Overview on, 35. *See also* Non-core curriculum
Musical intelligence, 13, 128

N

Naturalist intelligence, 13, 128
Newmann, F., 53
Non-core curriculum: acknowledging importance of, 27–28; Curriculum Overview on, 34–35; lack of formal reporting on, 24; portfolio contents on, 42

O

Observations: benefits of peer, 59–60; child's verbal expression of, 59–60; encouraging child's learning, 58–59

Outside language, 29, 30
Ownership. *See* Portfolio ownership

P

Parent Reflection Forms, 108
Parents: communication between schools and, 106–107; discussing standardized tests with, 104–105; invited to Portfolio Conference Evenings, 89–90; planning conversation between teachers and, 100–104; Portfolio archives reviewed by, 90, 92–93; reflection tag on sharing portfolios with, 98; sample invitation letter to, 91; taught to be part of Portfolio Conference, 99–109
Paulsen, L., 42
Paulsen, P., 42
Peer observations, 59–60
Physical Education: classroom portfolio video on, 94, 130; Curriculum Overview on, 35; portfolio contents on, 42. *See also* Non-core curriculum
Portfolio archive: creation of, 78–83; Portfolio Conference Evenings and use of, 88, 90, 92–93; student's review of, 66, 81–82
Portfolio Conference Evenings: as celebration, 126; children's attire during, 86; collaborative classroom video shown during, 94–96, 130; getting ready for, 88–89; inclusion facilitated by, 63–64; independent learning projects supported by, 65–66; inviting parents to, 89–90, 91; Learning Experiences Form used in, 30–33; Portfolio archive used during, 88, 90, 92–93; portfolio language to describe, 129; portfolios retrieved from archives for, 88; questions guiding structure of, 86–87; reflection tag on, 84; second graders self-evaluation of, 1–3; teaching parents to be part of, 99–109; traditional parent-teacher conference vs., 85–86
Portfolio culture/values, 124–130
Portfolio experience: fifth grade, 72–73; first grade, 69–70; fourth grade, 72; kindergarten, 68–69; second grade, 70–71; third grade, 71–72
Portfolio language: discovering the, 124–130; as key to portfolios, 120;

need for developing, 121–122; portfolio defined by, 122–124
Portfolio ownership: affirming child, 112–117; defining student vs. teacher, 43–44; interrelatedness of purpose/content and, 44–48, 128–129, 131; perspective of purpose/contents and, 48–49; portfolio language to describe, 128–129; stages of, 45
Portfolio purpose: discovering, 5, 6–9; interrelatedness of ownership/content and, 44–48, 128–129, 131; perspective of ownership/contents and, 48–49; portfolio language to describe, 128
Portfolio tasks, 40–41
Portfolios: assessment role of, 104–109; benefits of reflection tags to, 60–61; classroom video, 94–96, 130; as collection of child's work, 44; contents of, 42–43; as curriculum, 52; essence of, 130; first steps in compiling, 39–42; impact on standardized tests by, 132–133; individual needs of students and, 63–73; introduced to children, 56–59; language as key to, 120; lessons learned about, 131–133; motivational opportunities provided by, 55; multiple meanings/types of, 45–46. *See also* Reflection tags
Progress portfolio, 45–46
Prospect Center (Vermont), 2

R

Reardon, S., 51
Reflection concept: introducing students to, 58–59; peer observations enactment of, 59–60; portfolio language to describe, 129. *See also* Self-reflective language
Reflection tags: benefits to portfolio of, 60–61; on bonds between teachers, 22; on how children think of learning, 10; how to use, 50; on learning and school/classroom environment, 74; on ownership/purpose as key issues, 38; on Portfolio Conferences, 84; portfolio language to describe, 129–130; on potential of portfolios, 110; on sharing portfolios with parents, 98; supporting individual learning needs/interests, 62. *See also* Portfolios

Reporting forms: conference application of new, 30–33; designing new, 24–26. *See also* Learning Experiences Form

Roberts, M., 51

S

Scardamalia, M., 51, 54

School environment: impact on children by, 75–78; learning and created, 74; reflection tag on, 74. *See also* Learning environments

Schools: application of multiple intelligences model by, 13–15; communication between student home and, 106–107; designing new reporting form for, 24–26; learning and environment of, 74; organization of core/non-core curriculum, 15–16. *See also* Learning environments

Science Curriculum Overview, 34. *See also* Core curriculum

Second graders: Conference preparation for parents of, 103; portfolio experience, 70–71

Self-evaluation insights, 2–3

Self-reflective language: fourth grader's growing, 72; metacognition controlled through, 51; theory on promoting metacognition with, 53–56

Showcase portfolio, 45

Sizer, T., 53

Social Development Curriculum Overview, 35

Social Studies Curriculum Overview, 34. *See also* Core curriculum

Spanish: classroom portfolio video on, 94, 130; Curriculum Overview on, 35; portfolio contents on, 42. *See also* Non-core curriculum

Spatial intelligence, 13, 128

Spaulding, C., 55

Special needs students, 63–65

Spiritual intelligence, 13, 128

Staff development: activating multiple intelligences as, 26–27; portfolio contents activity as, 43

Standardized tests: accommodation of exclusion and, 64, 67; assessment using, 67–68; discussed with parents, 104–105; impact of portfolios on, 132–133; parent questions regarding, 121, 122

Stevenson, C., 43

Stories: Jeff's, 17–20; portfolio language definition of, 130; Tim's, 2–3, 5, 23

Students: abilities of, 11–15, 67–68; access to portfolio archives by, 66, 81–82; acknowledgment/approval from teacher to, 19–20; assessment of own learning by, 55–56; benefits of Portfolio Evenings to, 95–96; impact of school environment on, 75–78; introducing portfolios to, 56–59; "learning buddies" relationships among, 69, 88, 127; learning differences of, 67–68; learning to value all intelligences of, 13–15; metacognitive associations made by, 52; peer observations by, 59–60; reflective conversations with, 53–56; special needs, 63–65; substantive conversation with, 54; teaching through conversation of high school, 55. *See also* Child portfolio ownership; Individual learning needs

"Substantive conversation," 54

T

Tannen, D., 122

Teacher-and-child-organized portfolio, 46

Teacher-organized portfolio, 45

Teachers: acknowledgment/approval to child from, 19–20; connecting Gardner's theory to experiences of, 17–20; discovering portfolio purpose, 5, 6–9; home-school communication facilitated by, 109; inside vs. outside language of, 29–30; introducing portfolios to children, 56–59; learning to organize student portfolios, 39–42; multiple intelligences activated by, 26–27; planning conversation between parents and, 100–104; professional bonds between, 22; reflective conversation used by, 53–56

Teacher's conferences. *See* Portfolio Conference Evenings

Technology. *See* Library/Resource Center

Third graders: Conference preparation for parents of, 103; portfolio experience, 71–72

Tim's story, 2–3, 5, 23

Tyack, D., 117

V

Video (classroom portfolio), 94–96, 130

W

Washburne, C., 135, 136
Winnetka Public Schools: aesthetic development facilitated by, 140–141; background of, 135–136; basic skills taught in, 137–138; beliefs/educational objectives of, 136; child as total human being focus of, 138; citizenship preparation focus by, 140; intellectual growth concerns of, 137; physical/mental health fostered by, 139–140; professional culture of, 24; pursuit of excellence encouraged by, 141; response to individual child needs by, 138–139. *See also* Crow Island School
Witnessing the portfolio, 117–119
Wolf, D., 51